TONY ALCOSEBA

TONY ALCOSEBA

METAMORPHOSES

RAM MARTINEZ

Library of Congress Control Number: 2024919391

ISBN: 979-8-89228-250-5   (Paperback)
ISBN: 979-8-89228-249-9   (eBook)

Printed in the United States of America

For **Jose Tr. Alcoseba**
who showed me Art,

Ken M. Sanchez,
who taught me Philosophy,

and

Fr. Ro Salvaña,
who taught me the art of writing.

TABLE OF CONTENTS

LIST OF ILLUSTRATIONS

FOREWORD

It is with great pleasure that I introduce this abstract modern collection of works by Tony Alcoseba. As someone who has closely followed Tony's artistic journey, I have witnessed firsthand the evolution and maturation of his unique style. This book represents not just an anthology of his modern abstract paintings but a narrative of his life and inspirations.

Tony spent his childhood near Sanciangko Street and Jones Avenue. From the 1960s until the late 1980s, horse-drawn carriages called 'tartanilla' roamed the streets of Sanciangko, where his grandfather, Jose (Peping) Trinidad Alcoseba, had lived. Nowadays, tartanillas are just a distant memory. After retiring from his career as a school teacher, Peping Tr. Alcoseba, a UST Fine Arts graduate, provided drawing and painting lessons to wealthy children. He was a founding member of the Cebu Arts Association, together with Emilio Olmos, Silvestre Orfelia, Fidel Araneta, Ricardo Avila, Mel Tamayo, and Oscar Figuracion, from whom Tony drew some inspiration. It is Tony's personal desire to contribute to the cultural heritage through painting, capturing the sights and sounds of the city, and, more importantly, showcasing paintings that embody a distinctively Filipino identity.

My late father, Antonio Escario, owned several exquisite oil paintings by Tony Alcoseba. Among them, a beautiful oil landscape of the gardens at the Montebello Hotel graced our living room. While I am most familiar with Alcoseba's captivating oil and watercolor pieces, I have also had the pleasure of seeing a remarkable collection displayed at M Citi Suites, proudly curated by Atty. Jun Montuerto. Ram, a passionate collector of Tony Alcoseba's artworks, boasts an impressive array of the artist's pieces. As Tony's cousin, Ram shares a deep familial bond with the artist. Although they did not grow up together in the same household, they spent different periods of their lives together under the guidance of their grandfather. This unique personal connection provides Ram with profound insights into Tony's creative journey and artistic evolution.

This diverse collection of modern and abstract art is thoughtfully organized into five distinct groups, rather than by chronological periods. Spanning from the early 1980s to the present day, including the challenging era of the COVID-19 pandemic, this collection captures a wide range of themes and emotions.

The groups are as follows: 1. Fiesta (*Pista*) Series: vibrant and festive, these paintings encapsulate the joyous spirit of local Filipino celebrations and cultural festivities. 2. Beach Series: Inspired by the serene and dynamic coastal landscapes, these pieces evoke the tranquility and beauty not of the beach but of the beach goers. 3. Nomadic Series: This series explores the themes of movement and travel, reflecting the artist's fascination with the ever-changing world and the nomadic lifestyle of Badjaos. 4. Cat Series: Showcasing a variety of feline subjects, these paintings highlight the grace, mystery, and playfulness of cats. 5. Tartanilla Series: Capturing the charm of traditional horse-drawn carriages, these works pay homage to a Cebuano nostalgic mode of transportation and its cultural significance. Each series offers a unique perspective and insight into the artist's evolving style and thematic interests over the decades.

Compiling this collection was no easy feat. It was a difficult task to put all the paintings together and vet each one. Collating them and taking pictures was tedious, let alone talking to the current owners of the paintings and asking their permission to take photos. Gathering the correct dimensions and the materials used was an enormous task. It took more than two years to gather all these materials. This is why some paintings are untitled; the painter himself did not have an existing archival system. He had to rely on his memory to recall where the painting went, how much it sold for, and when it was sold. However, the purpose was not in the details of the value of the paintings but rather the art itself. Looking at the heart of the craft was more important than the monetary value of the paintings. Several beautiful paintings in private collections deserved to be showcased here. However, logistical challenges in obtaining permission prevented their inclusion.

Tony's journey is intricately linked to his early training in Western art, particularly in watercolor and oil. Yet, his inclination towards abstraction and modernism is also influenced by his colonial background. In works like "Nomadic Rhapsody" (2022) and the "Odyssey" (2022), Tony captures the essence of the southern Badjao tribes, using their cultural motifs as a vehicle for his swirling, abstract forms. This continuous movement reflects his belief in the endless possibilities of artistic expression, echoing Kandinsky's idea that art should evoke a spiritual response.

One of the most remarkable techniques Tony shares in this book is the "sperma technique." Gaining insight into this method is indeed welcoming and inspiring, encouraging others to innovate or polish their own techniques. This transparency not only showcases Tony's generosity as an artist but also his desire to contribute to the broader artistic community.

The "Tartanilla Series" exemplifies Tony's dedication to preserving his cultural heritage through art. Despite the challenges in locating and documenting these works, this series serves as a visual memoir, chronicling the vibrant life of Cebu during a bygone era. In the "Beach Series," Tony captures the serene beauty and dynamic interplay of light and water, evoking a sense of tranquility and timelessness. On the other hand, the "Cat Series" showcases his ability to infuse everyday scenes with whimsy and character, highlighting the grace and mystery of feline companions. Finally, the "Fiesta Series" bursts with color, energy, and movement reflecting the joyous celebrations and rich traditions of Filipino culture.

This book is dedicated not only to the arts but also to the enduring bond of friendship. The author and I once shared an idyllic and innocent time as prenovices of the Jesuits. Our paths diverged as I pursued my studies at Xavier University, while Ram attended the Ateneo in Manila. In time, we embraced the wisdom of relinquishing our religious aspirations, which allowed our friendship to flourish. We reconnected as writers for the local Cebu daily, The Freeman Sunday magazine. I began as an opinion writer and rose to the position of editor, serving from 1994 to 2000, before moving briefly to the Davao Catholic Herald in 2021. Concurrently, Ram became a contributing writer for the Independent Post and Cebu Daily News, while sharing his knowledge as an educator at various local universities.

As you delve into this collection, you will not only witness the artistic evolution of Tony Alcoseba but also gain a deeper understanding of the cultural and historical contexts that shaped his work. This book is a testament to Tony's enduring commitment to his craft and his desire to share his unique vision with the world.

Vince V. Escario

PREFACE

I grew up in a two-story multi-generational home where my patriarchal grandfather, Jose Tr. Alcoseba, a painter, was at the center of our family life. Three other families lived there too. The house I remember was filled with paintings, its walls adorned with numerous artworks that we often took for granted. The first floor was where my aging grandfather always sat in a very old chair. I never saw him leave that chair except to eat in our large, messy dining hall, which had one common refrigerator. Day in and day out, he painted, and on Sundays, children from wealthy families would come to learn how to draw or paint from him. Looking back, I can only imagine the years I spent growing up in that house.

In 1977, a big fire broke out and destroyed the entire block of Sanciangko and Junquera Street, including our house. What happened to the paintings? No one thought of them. We moved south, near Pardo, where my grandfather continued to paint until his twilight years. I recall my mother bringing only one painting, a collage portrait of him. Years later, I acquired a landscape oil painting of my grandfather from my aunt, "The Fire Tree" (1968), which now adorns our current home. I have always wished I had taken more of those paintings with me. Even after the fire, his paintings were scrupulously sold by some agents.

During my adult years, I became more interested in art and started collecting watercolor paintings by Tony, who began gaining popularity at that time. Tony, the son of my mother's elder brother, and I grew close during this period. I followed his work and wrote several short articles about him. It has been a long dream of mine to someday write about Tony. Hence, this book.

R.A.M.

METAMORPHOSES

by Ram Martinez

THE VISION AND ATTITUDE

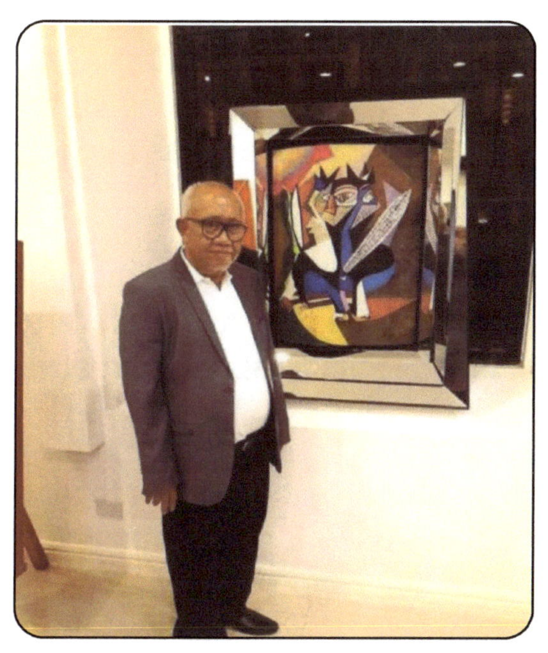

TONY ALCOSEBA first sold a painting at Christie's (Hong Kong) in 1986. During this period, he sought to explore new techniques and artistic ventures. His recent works can be traced back to this time, as his style and brushstrokes remain consistent with his earlier watercolor and oil pieces. His evolution is reminiscent of how Picasso and Braque introduced their first collages, a pivotal moment in the development of Cubism.

Cubism is aimed to examine forms devoid of traditional emotions, with Braque's reductive style contributing significantly to the modernist art movement. Tony must have grown tired of watercolor painting after securing several wins in competitions. He seemed to grapple with balancing illusion and realism which eventually led him to create a sense of three-dimensional imagery in his work.

Cubism has long been established by the masters as a format showcasing vision and attitude. While it was revolutionary in the time of Picasso and Braque, it is no longer groundbreaking today. What sets Tony apart is his innovative 3-faces technique, which infuses his work with a distinct, revolutionary quality. What remains to be seen is how Tony's vision and attitude will continue to shape his artistic journey.

Tony's vision is to pioneer a bold new era in the world of contemporary art, guided by a relentless pursuit of self-expression, innovation, and cultural legacy. In 2015 and 2017 he joined an exhibit at Qube gallery. Drawing from his rich background and experiences, Tony seeks to transcend conventional boundaries, forging a path that merges artistic exploration with profound introspection.

Driven by a desire to challenge the status quo, Tony's artistic journey embodies a fusion of tradition and modernity that weaves together the threads of his colonial heritage with the vibrant tapestry of Filipino identity. The Fiesta (Pista) series is a testament of his own personal experience.

With each stroke of his brush, he captures the essence of his surroundings and infuses his creations with the sights, sounds, and emotions of his homeland.

At the heart of Tony's vision lies a commitment to authenticity and depth, as he navigates the complexities of abstractionism and modernism with unwavering resolve. By embracing the nomadic spirit of artistic exploration, he ventures into uncharted territories and seeks to unravel the mysteries of existence and consciousness through his art.

Tony envisions a world where his paintings serve as portals to new realms of thought and emotion. He invites viewers to embark on a transformative journey of self-discovery. With each masterpiece, he inspires, provokes, and ultimately, ignites a spark of creative awakening in the hearts and minds of all who encounter his work.

In pursuit of this vision, Tony remains steadfast in his dedication to excellence, integrity, and his personal promise to pursue artistic truth. Through his unwavering commitment to craft and vision, he aims to leave an indelible mark on the landscape of contemporary art and shapes the cultural discourse of generations to come.

Tony's attitude towards his craft is one of unwavering passion and relentless pursuit of excellence. Rooted in a deep appreciation for tradition and cultural heritage, he approaches each canvas with a sense of reverence that infuses his work with the soulful resonance of his experiences.

In his book, *Kamingaw* (2017), art historian and painter Raymund Fernandez quotes Cebuano painter Martino Abellana who once enthused *"that there's more to an artist than sketching, drawing, painting, or sculpting; that there's more to an artist than the paintings they create."*

Yet, beneath this reverence lies an irrepressible spirit of innovation and experimentation that drives Tony to push the boundaries of artistic expression beyond convention.

With a poet's sensitivity and a conductor's precision, he orchestrates his compositions with a keen eye for detail and an intuitive understanding of form and color. Guided by a profound sense of purpose, Tony embraces the challenges of abstractionism and modernism with a tenacity that borders on obsession, determined to leave an indelible mark on the canvas of contemporary art.

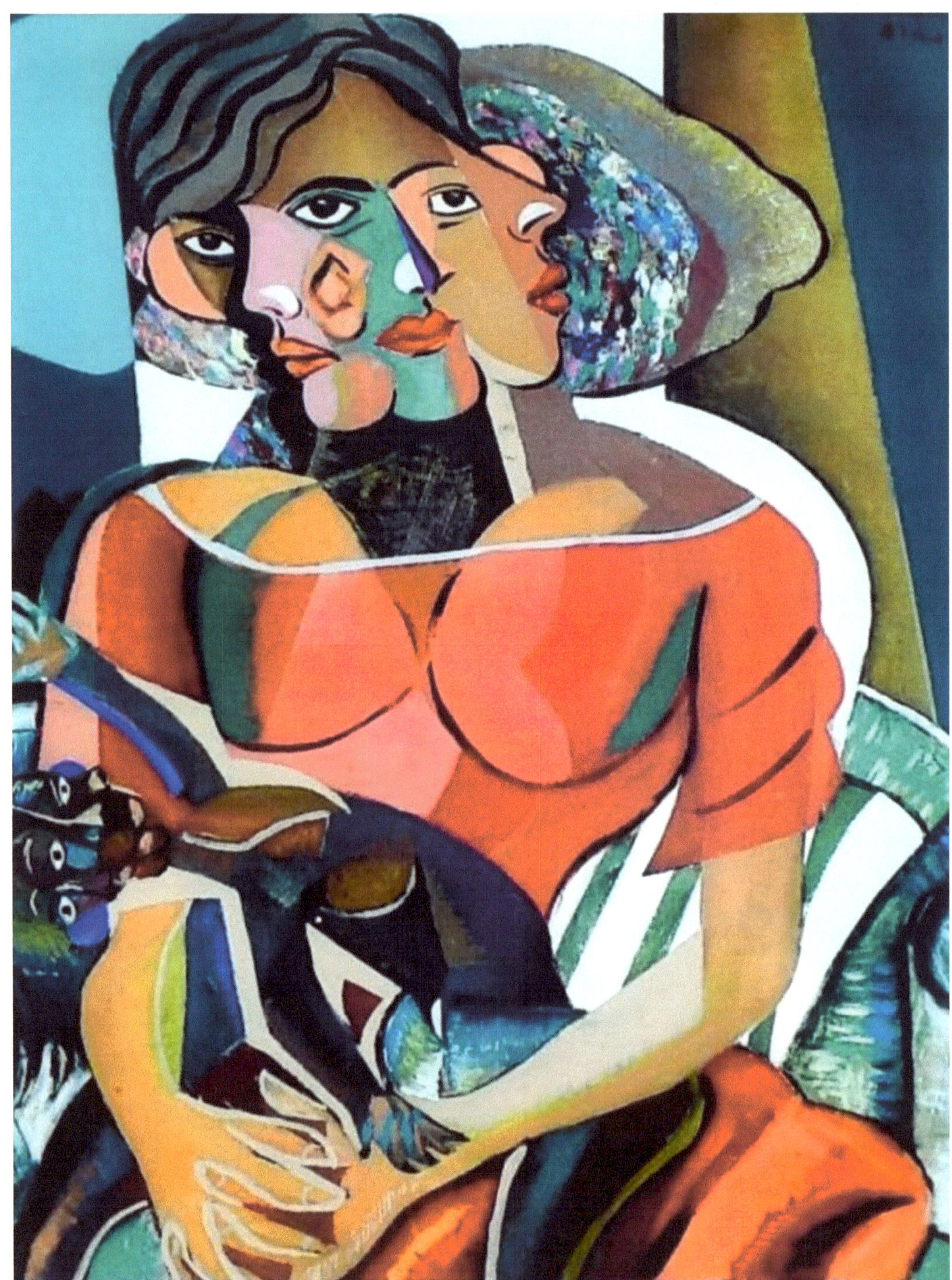

Prostitute, 2019, 22 x 30 in, acrylic on board, collection of Atty. Julito Alvarez.

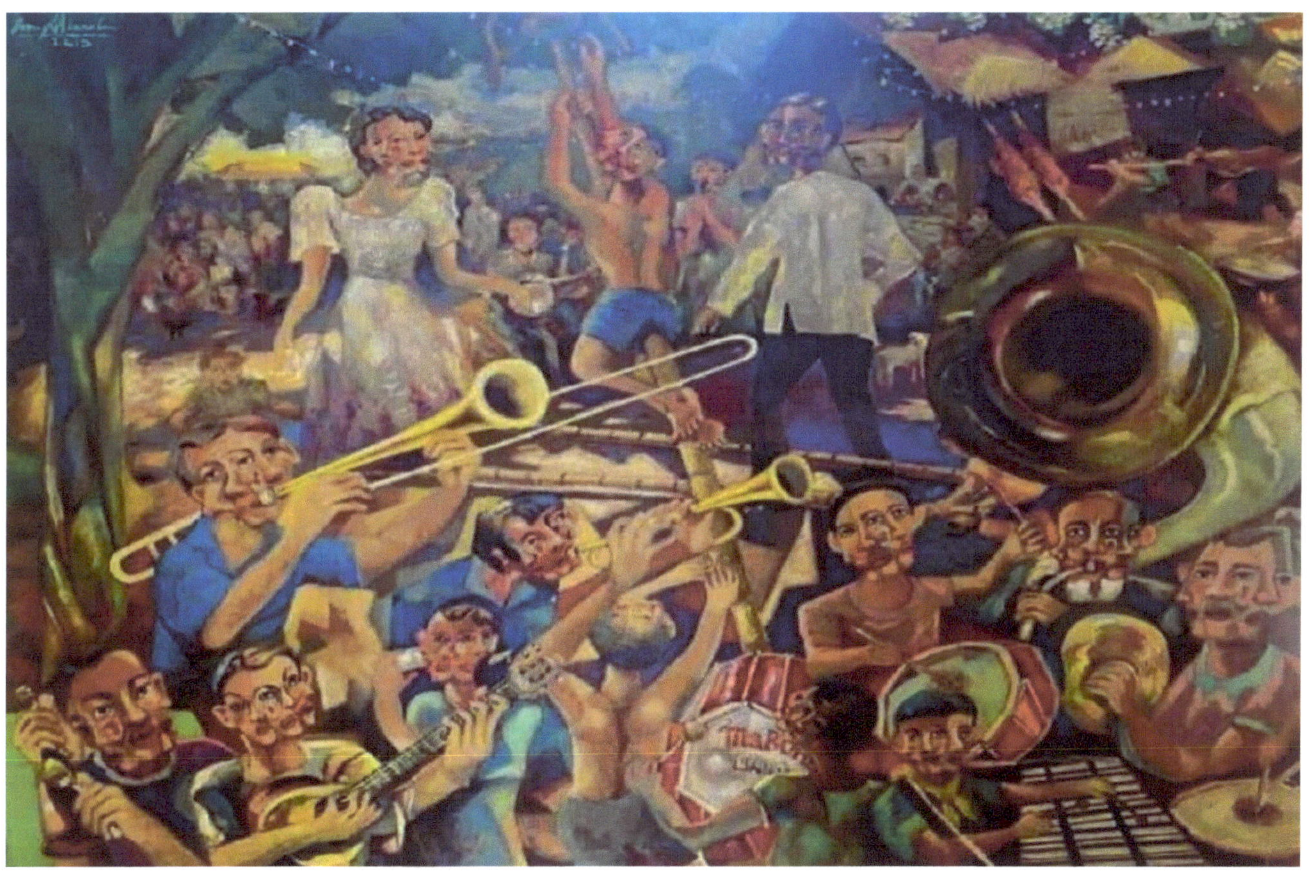

Fiesta Series #1, Bisperas sa Pista: Kalingawan, 2015, 107 x 137 cm acrylic on canvas, collection of Atty. Regal Oliva.

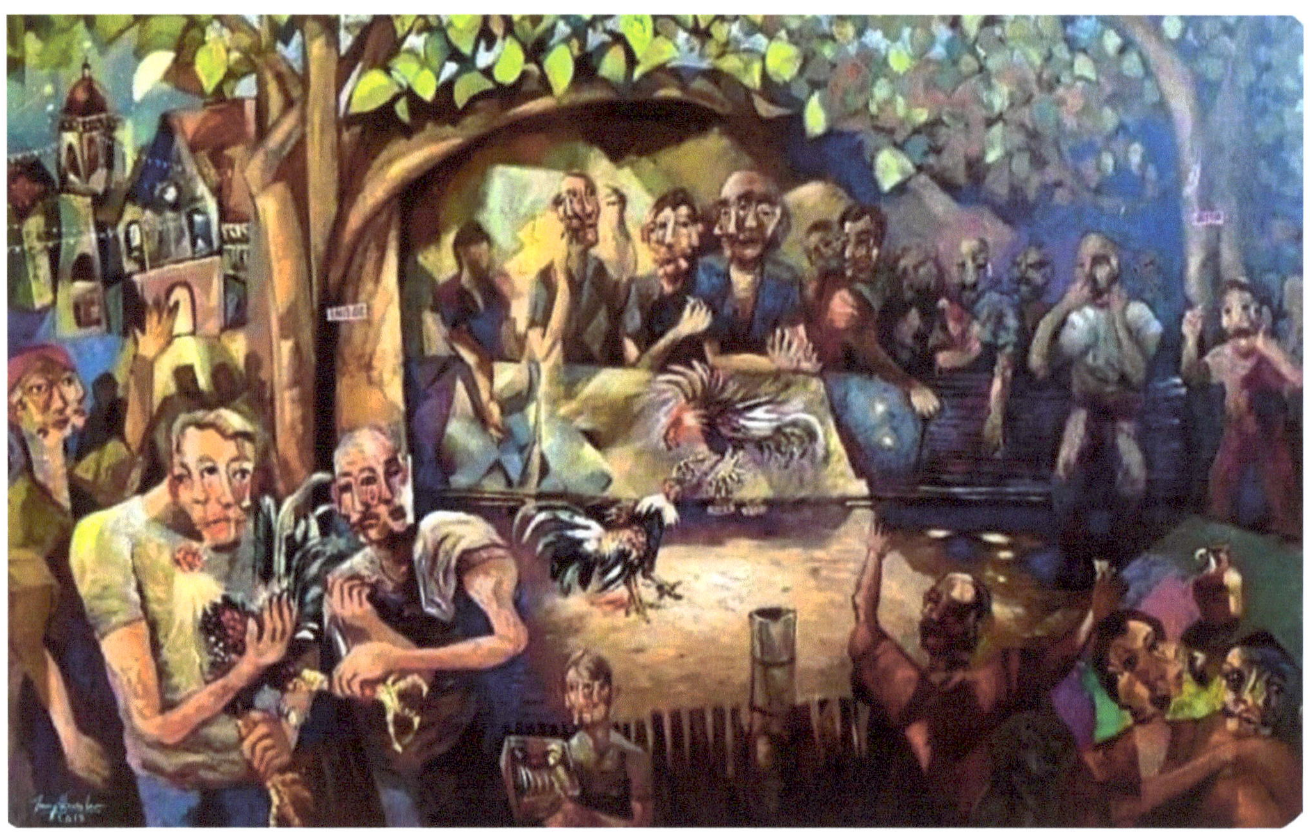

Fiesta Series #2, Bisperas sa Pista: Tigbakay sa Barrio, 2015, 107 x 137 cm, acrylic on canvas, collection of Atty. Regal Oliva.

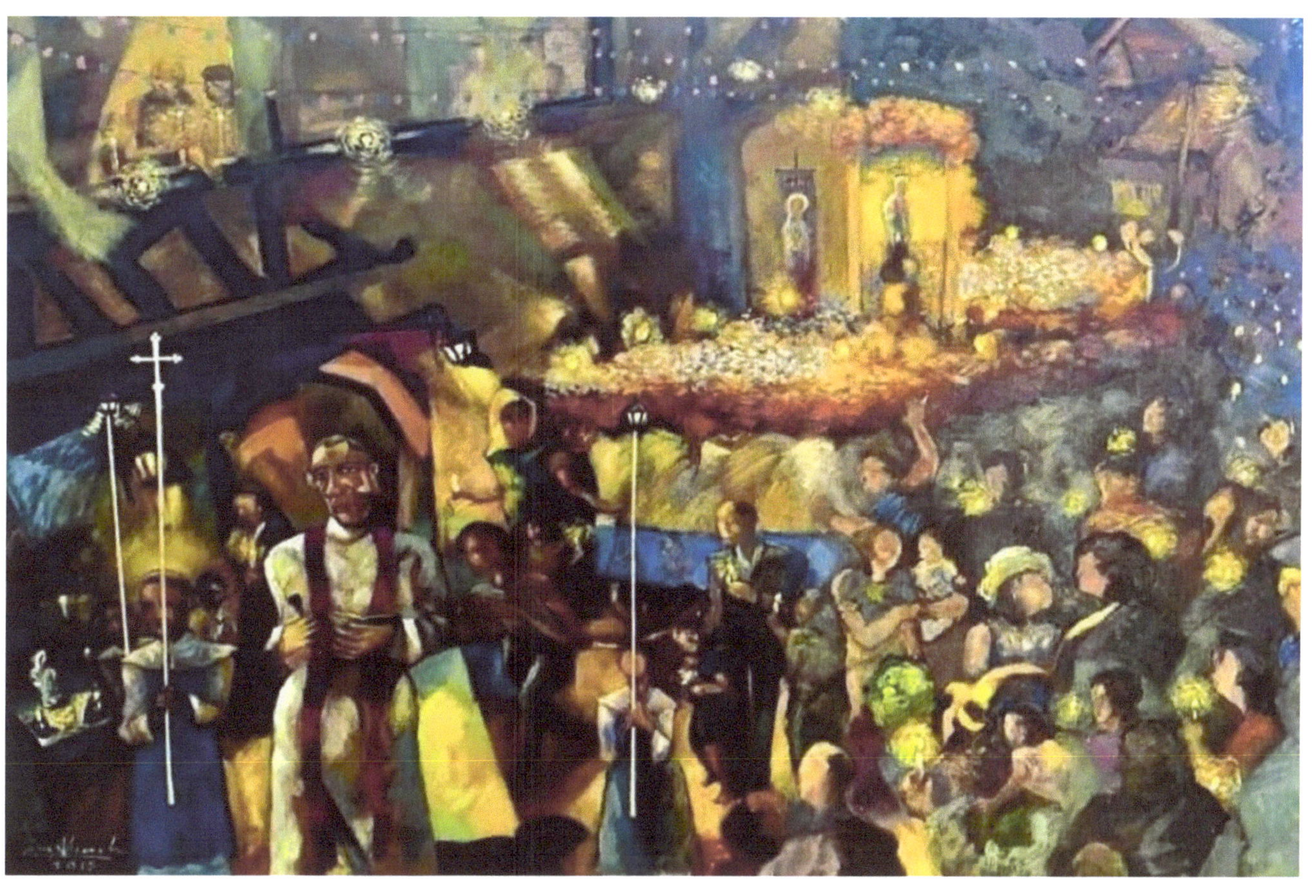

Fiesta Series #3, Bisperas sa Pista: Pangilin sa Patron, 2015, 107 x 137 cm, acrylic on canvas, collection of Atty. Regal Oliva.

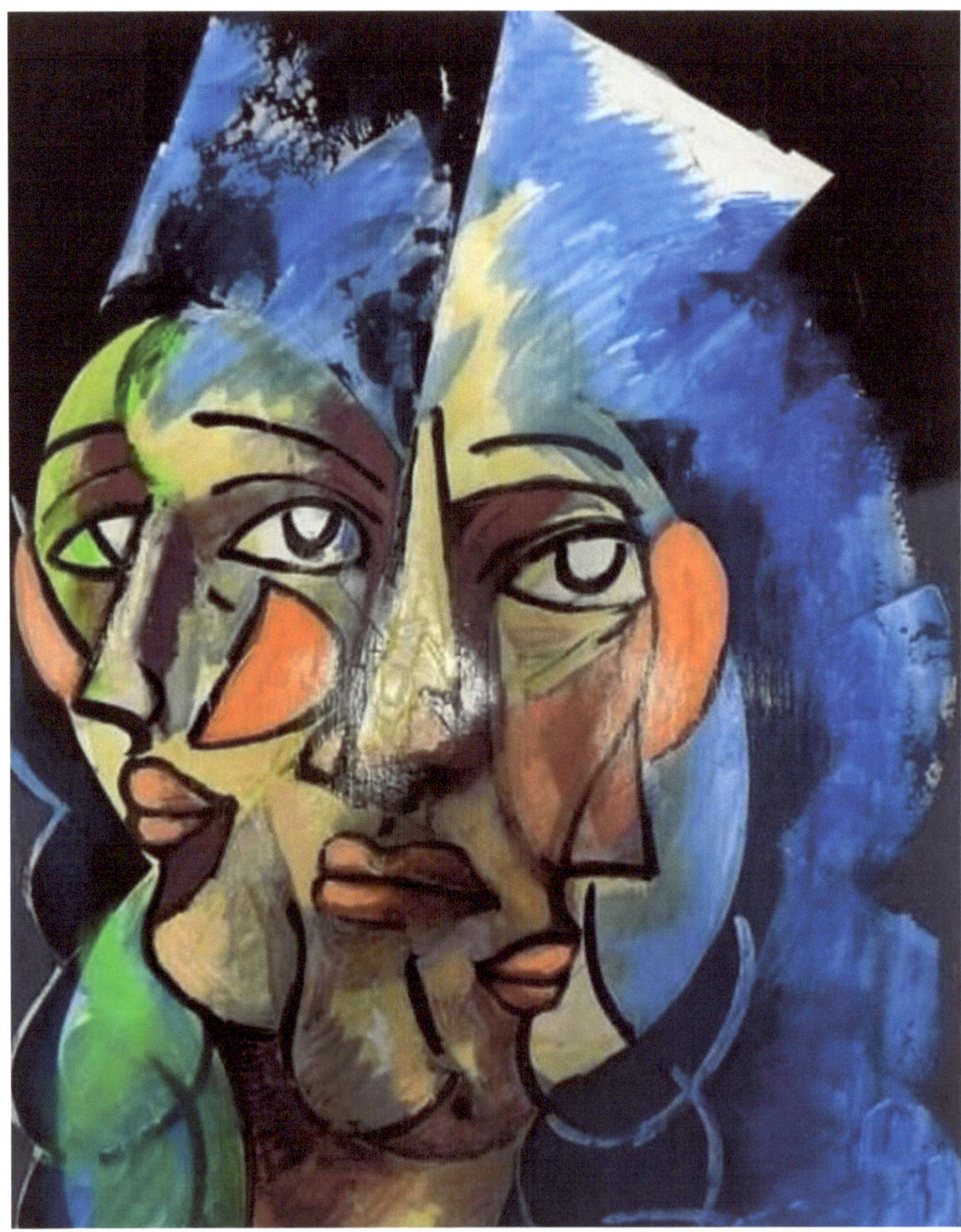

Untitled, 2021, 22 x 30 in, acrylic on board.

BADJAO INFLUENCE: A PRELUDE TO THE NOMADIC SERIES

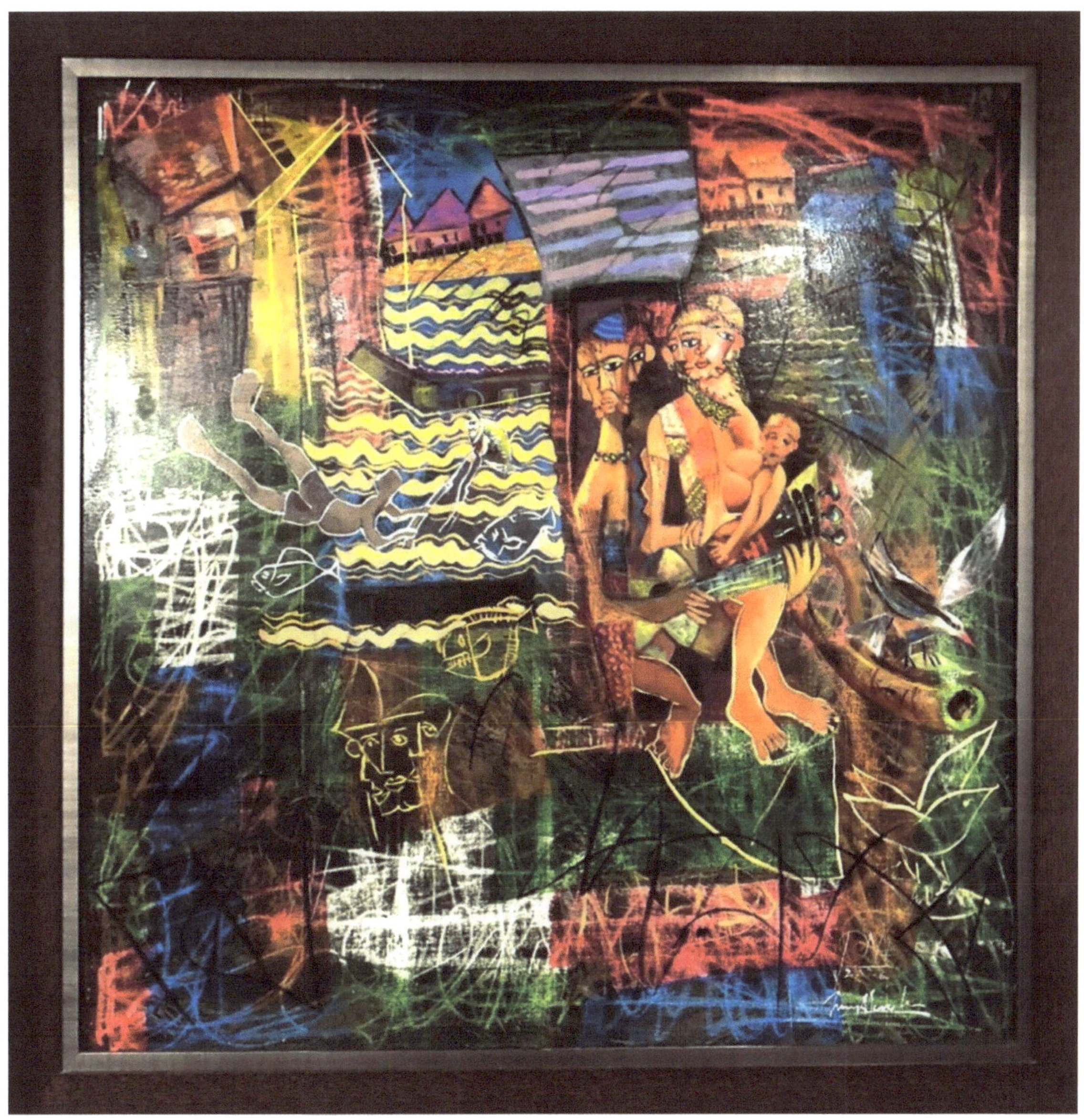

Meandering of Badjaos, 2022-2024, 4 x 4 ft, acrylic on canvas.

PLOT, according to Aristotle, stands as the foundational essence, the very heartbeat of tragedy, while character assumes a supporting role. Analogously, in the realm of painting, Aristotle suggests that randomly splashing a surface with the finest colors would pale in comparison to the meticulous outlining of a picture. Appreciating Tony's life and the historical context enriches our understanding of his art, offering a glimpse into the intricate narrative of its creation. Tony's recent body of work appears to falter in encapsulating the desired aesthetic allure or transformative essence he seeks to convey. That is because, in his own words, "these ideas and the technique take time to form."

They unfold as a symphonic journey in progress, a canvas that echoes with the rhythms of self-discovery rather than a static masterpiece. This exploration seems to mirror a quest to unearth the depths of his soul by transcending the mere pursuit of visual beauty.

Tony's artistic wanderlust, reminiscent of the nomadic traditions of the Badjao people, sees him navigating through uncharted creative territories, perpetually in search of new vistas and insights.

Technique, while still vital, takes a backseat to the raw emotion and profound introspection palpable in his oeuvre, underscoring his quest to break free whatever binds him to nature, from artistic conventions that now allow him to express his innermost truths with unwavering authenticity. His works beyond the 1980's serve as a bold proclamation of self-expression, immune to external judgments or monetary considerations.

This, in essence, represents Tony's personal *"carpe diem"* moment, a fearless challenge he sets for himself to redefine the boundaries of artistic expression.

Amidst this contemplation, one cannot help but ponder: if plot is the soul of tragedy, then what defines the essence of painting? For Tony his art transcends the mere replication of optical stimuli; it is a continuous evolution of self-discovery and expression, an intricate dance in the boundless realms of color, line, and form.

While his earlier works of watercolor and oil depicted life-like scenes, his current artistic odyssey embodies a departure towards modernism, a gradual metamorphosis marked by bold strokes and conceptual innovations over time.

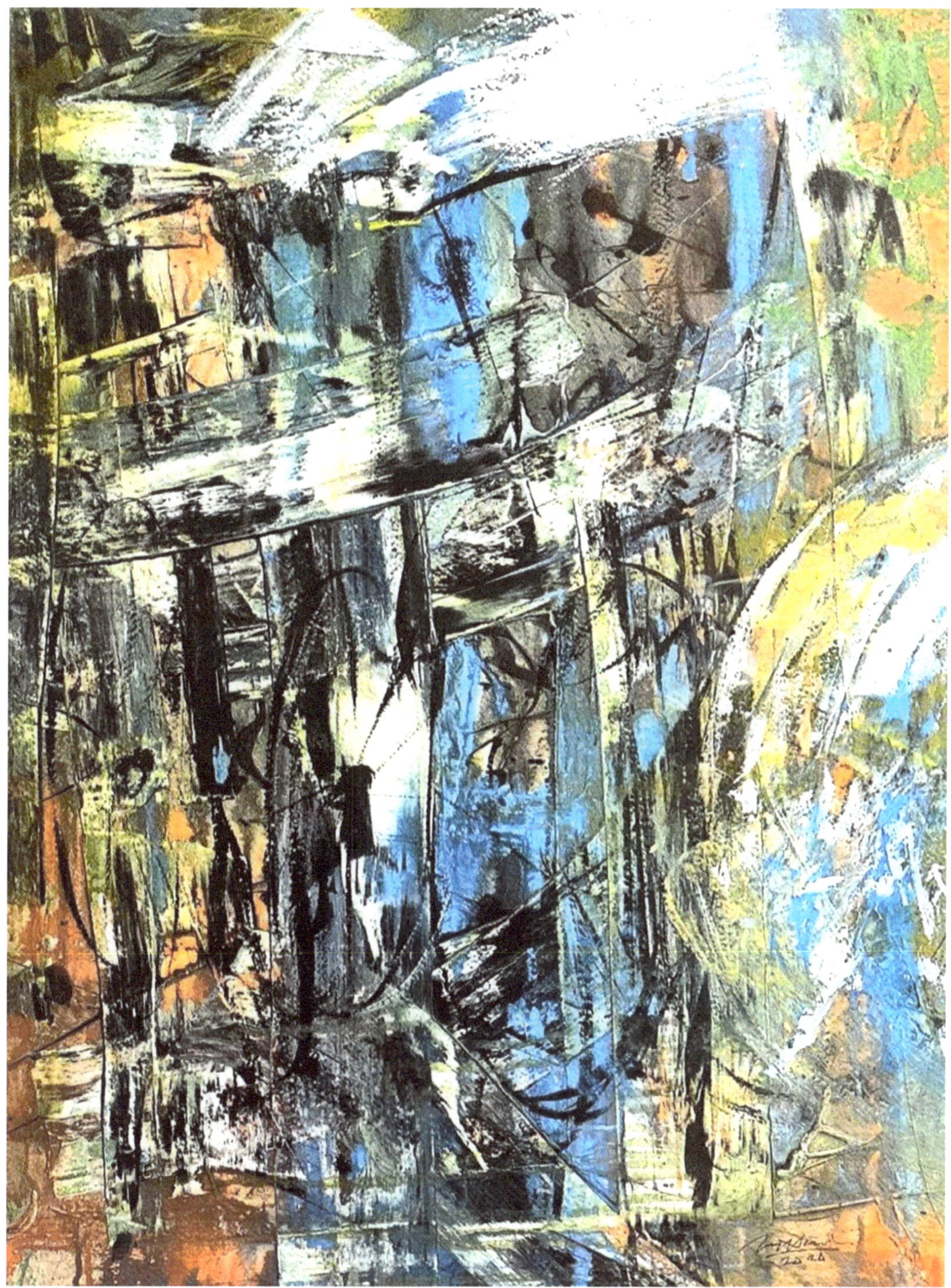

Organized Chaos, 2020, 18 x 26 in, acrylic on board, collection of
Dr. Richard Myles Montesclaros.

THE CAT: 3-FACED IMAGERY

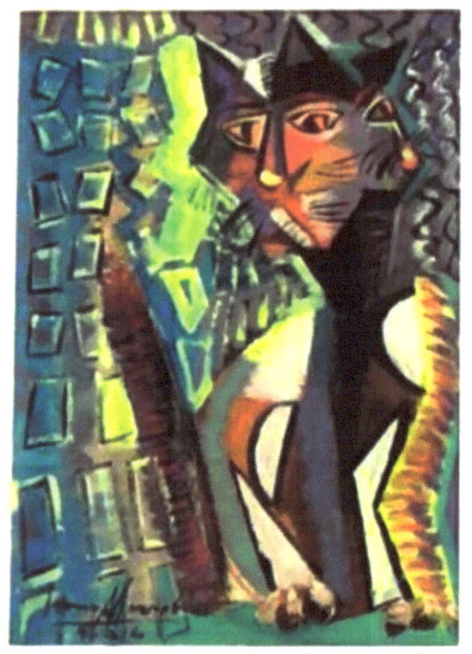

Cat Series, 2016, 18 x 30 in, acrylic on board, photo c. 2023, collection of Roy Martinez, Johnson City, TN.

IT must be noted that Tony began to break free from the constraints of nature when he initially lacked the direction and focus to venture into abstraction. This was gradual process that he understood well. Nevertheless, he persevered and continued to move forward.

It all began with the cats. Taking a nostalgic stroll down memory lane, he revisited his past architectural drafts and explored both symmetrical and asymmetrical renditions. His first attempt, *El Gato* in 1986, left him ecstatic and inspired to perfect his technique. The subject of the cat brought him immense joy in his newfound approach. However, when he attempted to depict the human figure, much to his delight, with its demanding symmetry, he faced greater challenges compared to the feline subjects.

He noted some discrepancies in achieving perfect harmony, particularly with the human face, which he found difficult to express as he desired. As an artist, it pained him. He encountered inconsistencies, as he described them that marked this period as a difficult transition in his artistic journey.

He aimed to achieve the same level of expression and perfection as he did with the cats, albeit facing greater complexities with human subjects.

Tony grappled with the unique challenge of having to express the intricacies of the human form through geometric abstraction. While mastery of this style is evident in his portrayal of subjects like cats, translating the human anatomy into geometric shapes posed significant hurdles. The bilateral symmetry of cats served as an ideal canvas for Tony's experimentation. That allowed him to explore lines and forms with greater precision. However, when it came to depicting the human figure, Tony encountered complexities that defied easy resolution.

Unlike cats, humans lack the inherent symmetry that lends itself to geometric abstraction. The "3- faces" technique he employs further complicates matters as it requires a delicate balance between artistic interpretation and anatomical accuracy.

Is it really possible to make an abstraction of the human face with a humane touch?

Tony explores the depths of deconstruction and unravels its complexities with sensitivity and artistry which can be seen clearly through this *Nude 2013* painting of a woman. Through his innovative approach, he distills the essence of humanity into a series of geometric forms and patterns which when gleamed from different angles, shows some form of movement. Take for example his beach series. This particular body of work maybe likened to different songs with almost the same chorus lines. This invariably invites the viewer to contemplate of the beauty of the human form through a prism of abstraction.

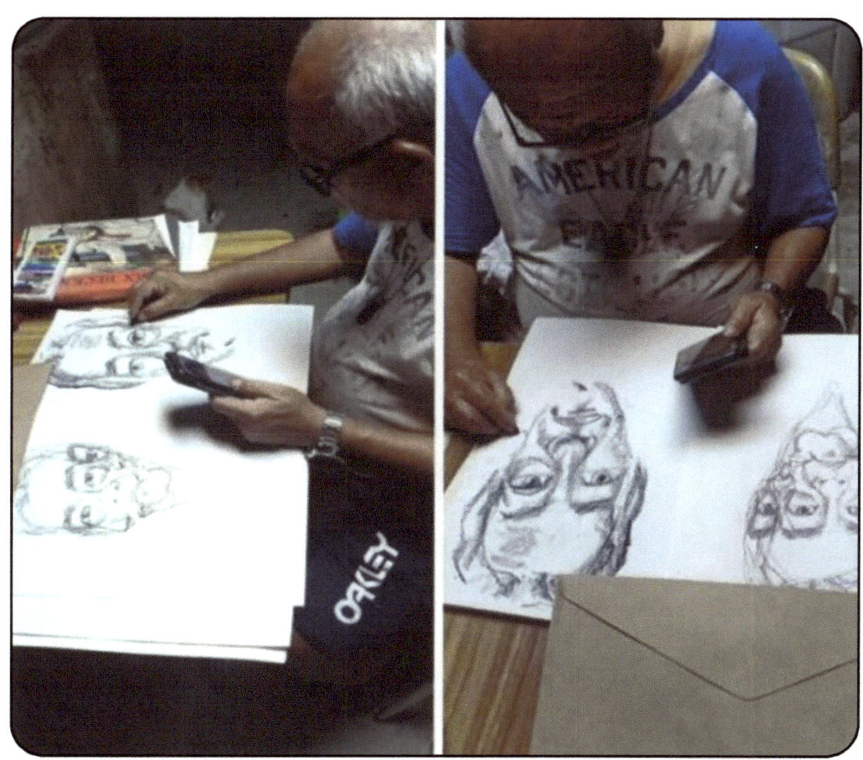

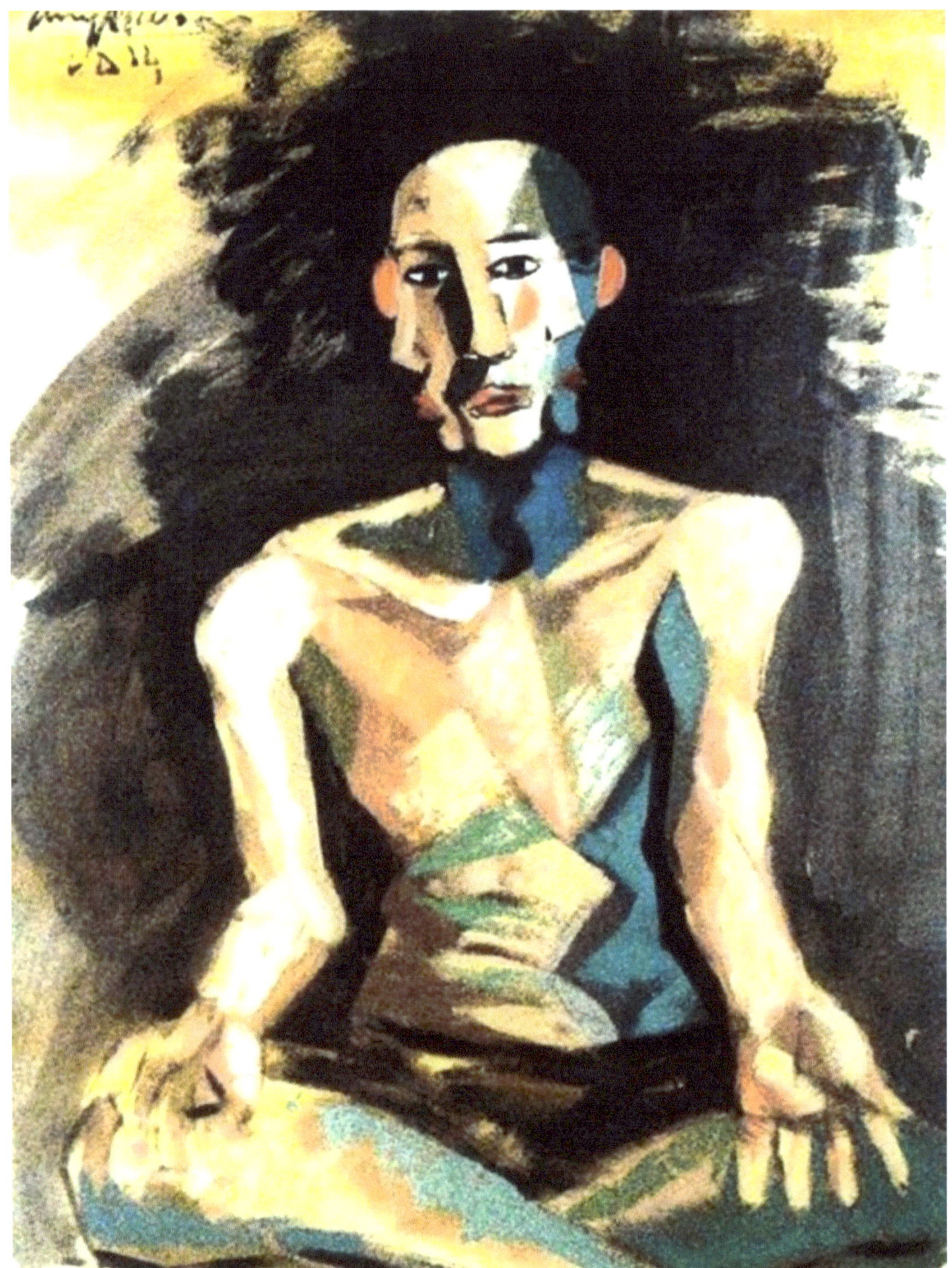

The Meditation, 2012, 22 x 30 in, acrylic on board, collection of Atty. Ramon Esguerra.

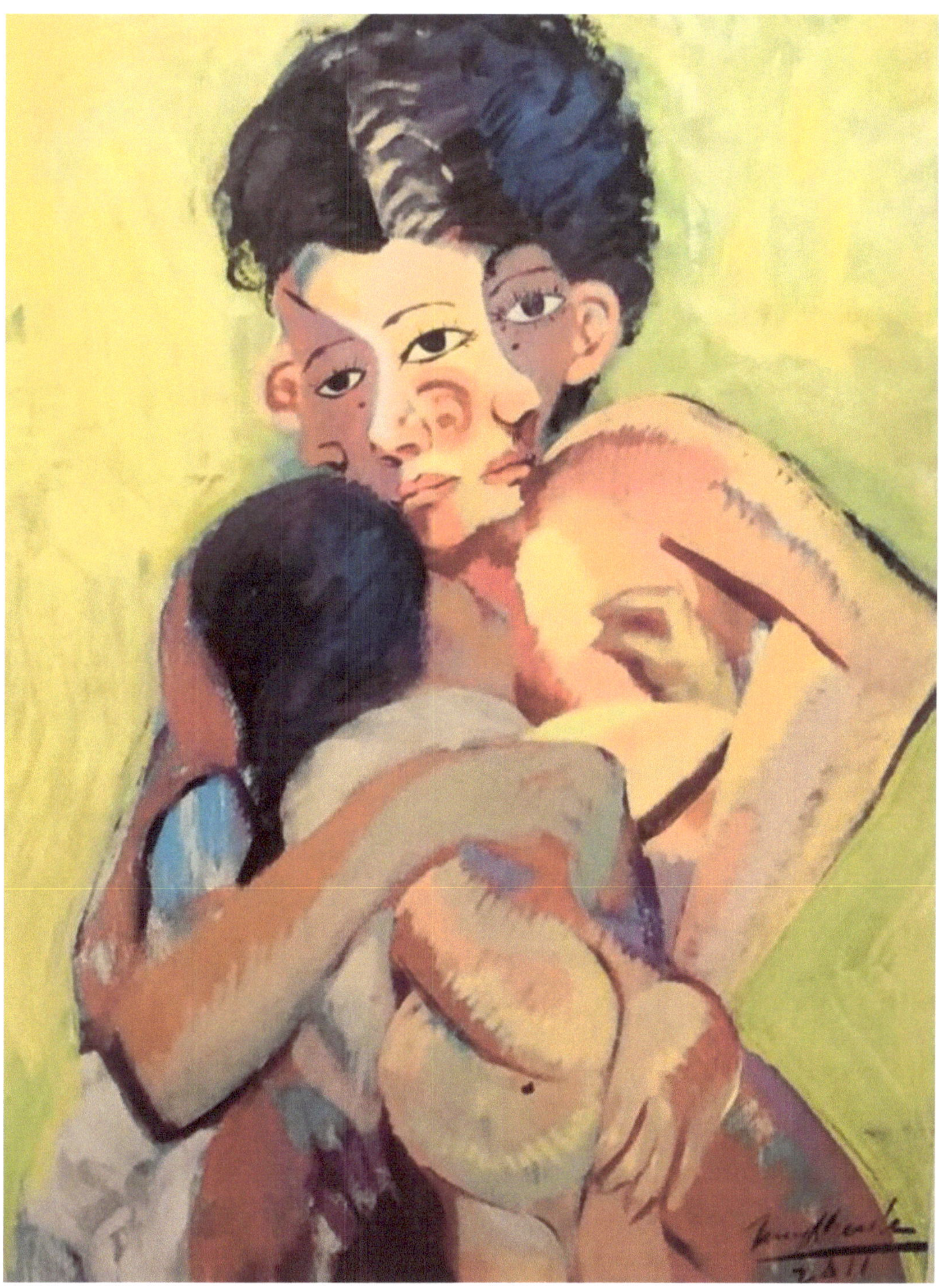

Mother and Child, 2011, 20 x 30 in, acrylic on board.

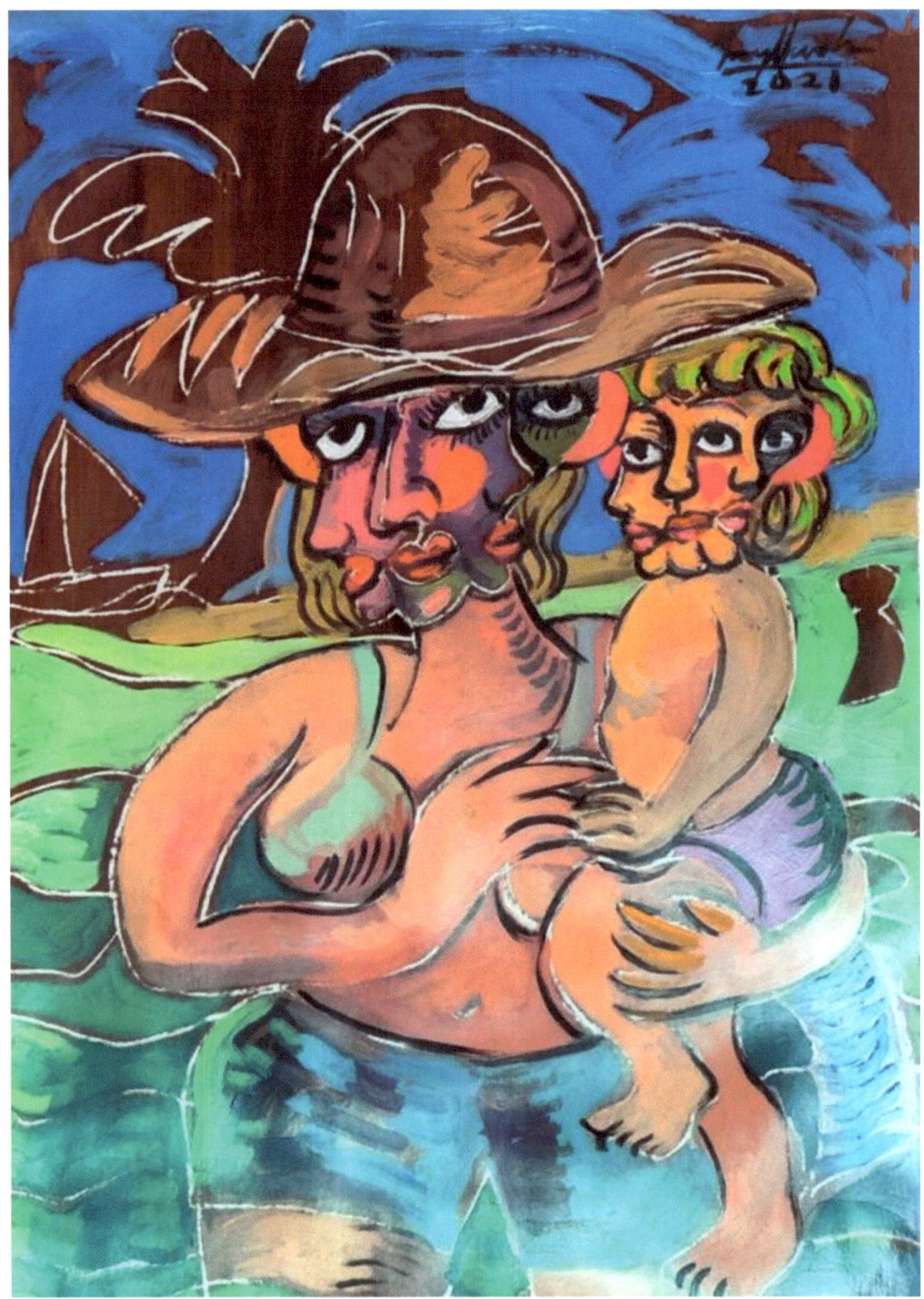

Beach Series #1: Family at the Beach, 2021, 22 x 30 in, acrylic on board, collection of Ken M. Sanchez, Fairfield, CA.

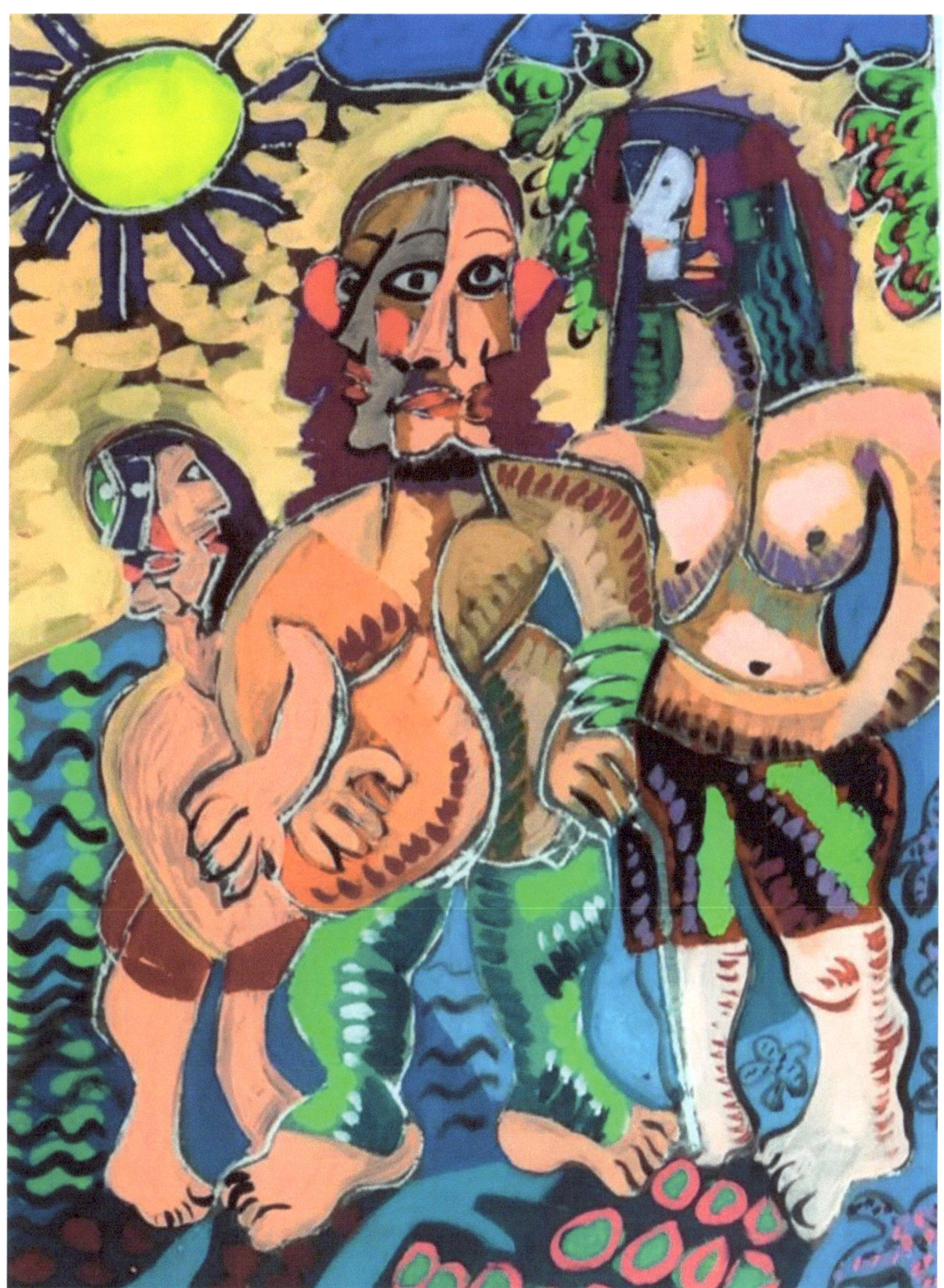

Beach Series #2: Family at the Beach, 2021, 22 x 30 in, acrylic on board.

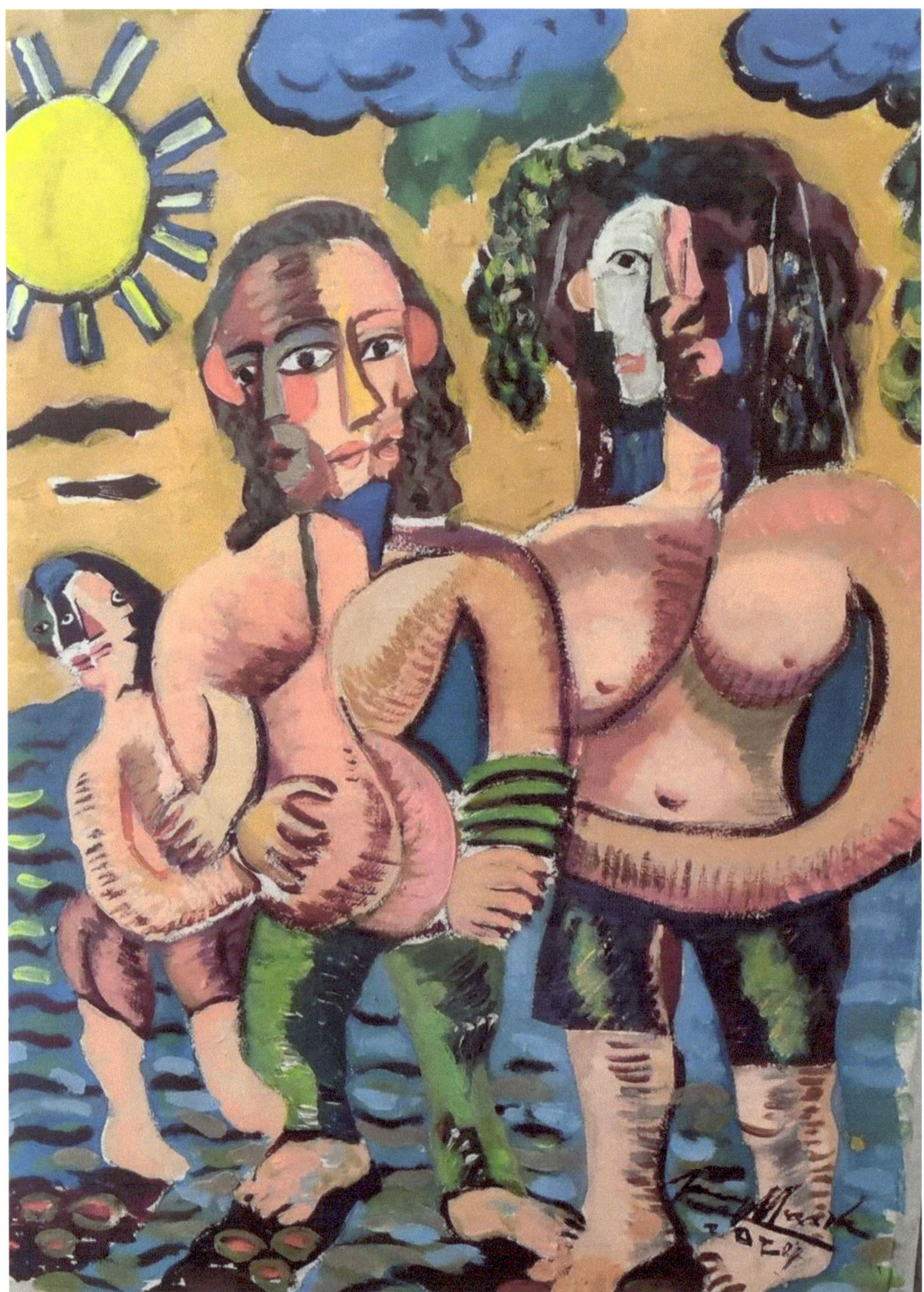

Beach Series #3: *Family at the beach*, 2024, 22 x 30 in, acrylic on board, collection of Ken M. Sanchez, Fairfield, CA.

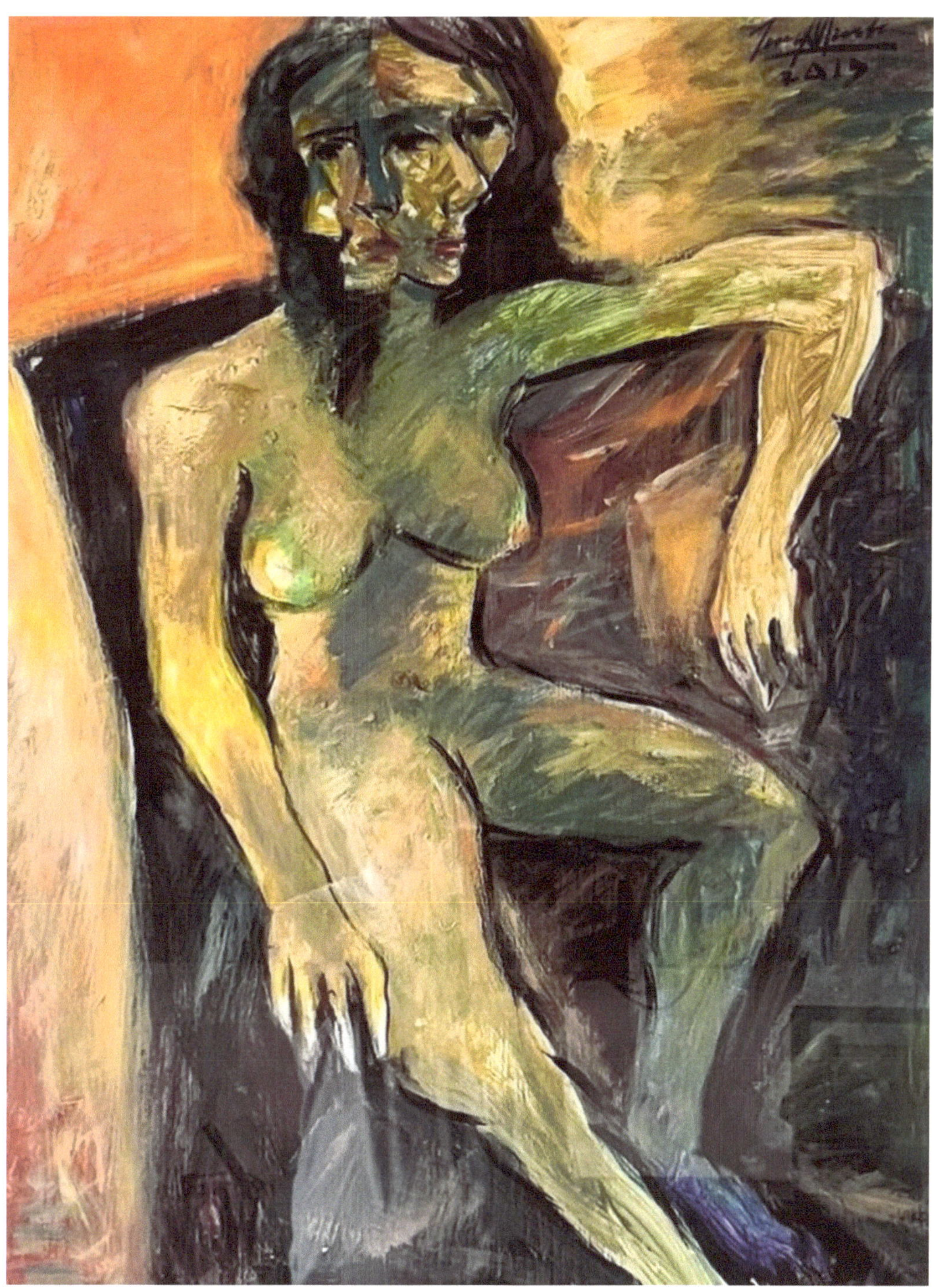

Nude, 2013 , 20 x 29 in, acrylic on board.

SYMPHONIC ABSTRACTION: A UNION OF LINES AND FORMS; AN OVERTURE TO THE NOMADIC SERIES

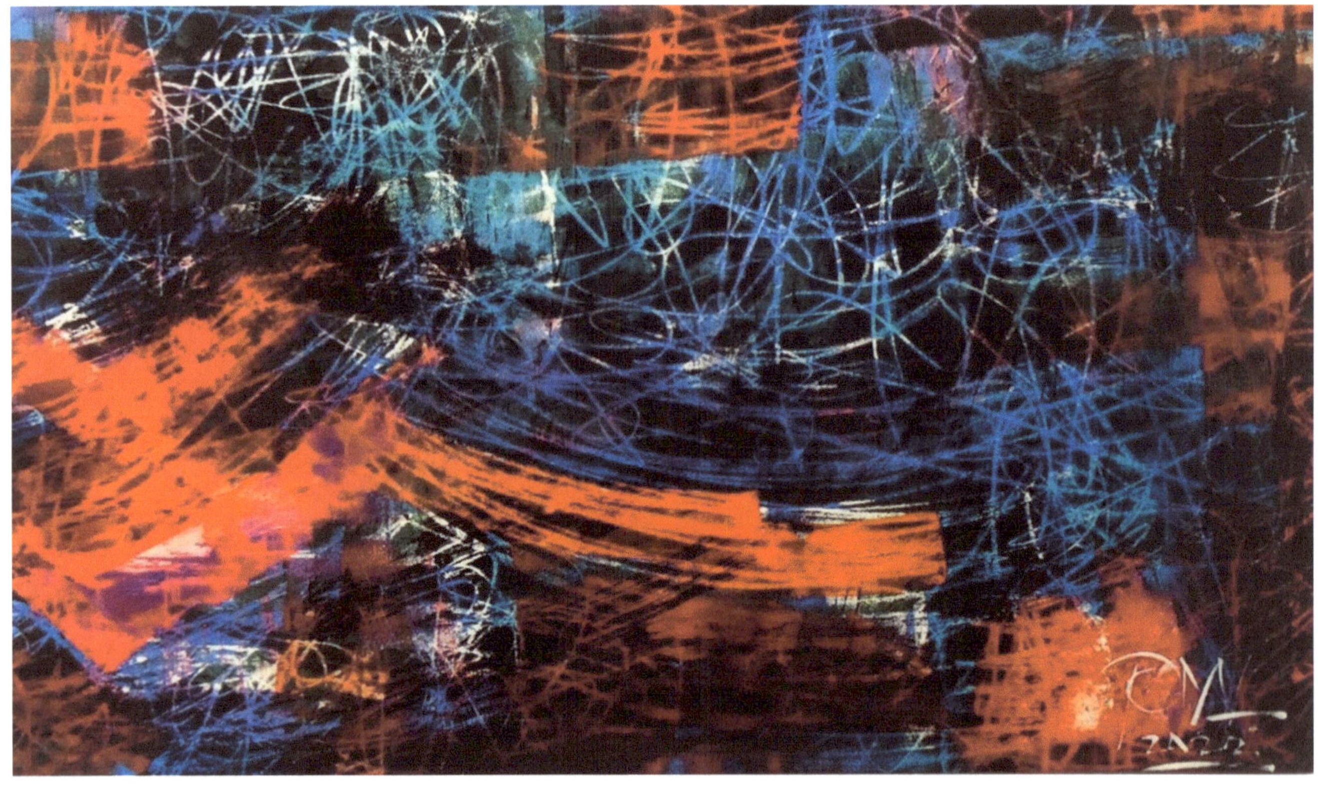

Nomadic series #1: Odyssey, 2022, 4 x 8 ft, acrylic on wood, private collection of the author.

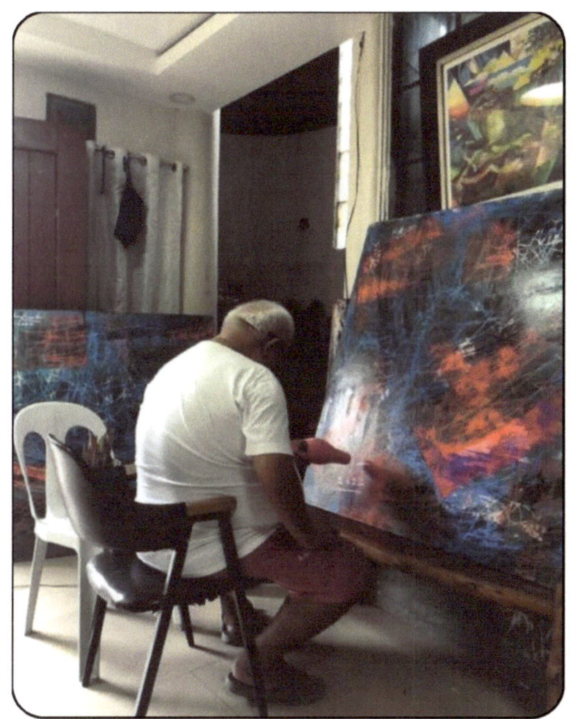

AFTER 2021 Tony started to produce paintings with a new conceptual approach to his work. He called this *symphonic abstraction*.

Inspired by a rich tapestry of music, Tony thus began to orchestrate a symphony of colors, shapes, and textures that until today still captivates the imagination and stirs the soul.

Through symphonic abstraction, Tony's approach was to channel the harmonious rhythms and dynamic interplay of musical motifs into his visual creations. Not unlike a conductor leading an orchestra, Tony managed to deftly combine disparate elements into a cohesive expressive whole that weaved together a symphony of form and color.

In due time, Tony's symphonic abstraction proved to be his captivating overture that laid the foundation for the mesmerizing crescendo of his innovative Nomadic Series. This set the stage for the introduction of Tony's trademark of the Sperma technique. (More on the sperma technique in the succeeding chapter.)

By building on his symphonic abstraction using his sperma technique, Tony navigated the intricate contours of human migration and survival by distilling its essence into a series of geometric shapes and patterns that within a short period of time flourished into a staggering number of art works. This proved to be not only a most productive time in Tony's artistic career but also was a most challenging period of taking greater risks in terms of artistic experimentation.

While Tony used his sperma technique on canvas he was also emboldened to experiment the use of lawanit[1] wood, a material that was never thought of to be a viable alternative. While Tony's success on his work with lawanit wood[1] remains to be seen, the fact that he discovered both a new technique and a viable option to canvas proves him to be a distinct revolutionary and modern artist.

---

[1] Lawanit is made from wood chips/shavings mixed with glue and rolled out in the form of a sheet like plywood.

Within a year or so, he was able to create at least 10 huge works. Other than just being unusually productive and experimental in terms of technique and material he also began to work with pieces that were much larger than his usual works.

Take for example the Odyssey originally at 4ftx8ft was a huge painting to hang. It required a wide wall space for proper display. So that towards the end of 2023, it was cut into two individual pieces.

Also during this time Tony made an important decision as he was progressing and discovering new facets to his artistry and that was to change the way he would sign his pieces from then on instead of signing it with the usual Tony Alcoseba to TONAL.

This was indicative of the major upheavals occurring in the man.

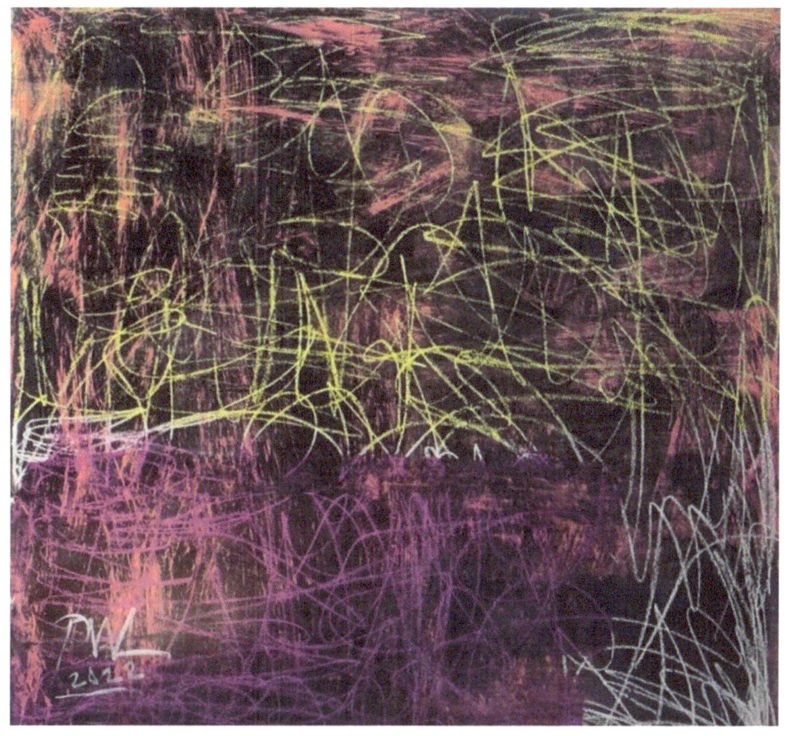

Nomadic Series #2: Sound of Silence, 2022, 4 x 4 ft, acrylic on wood.

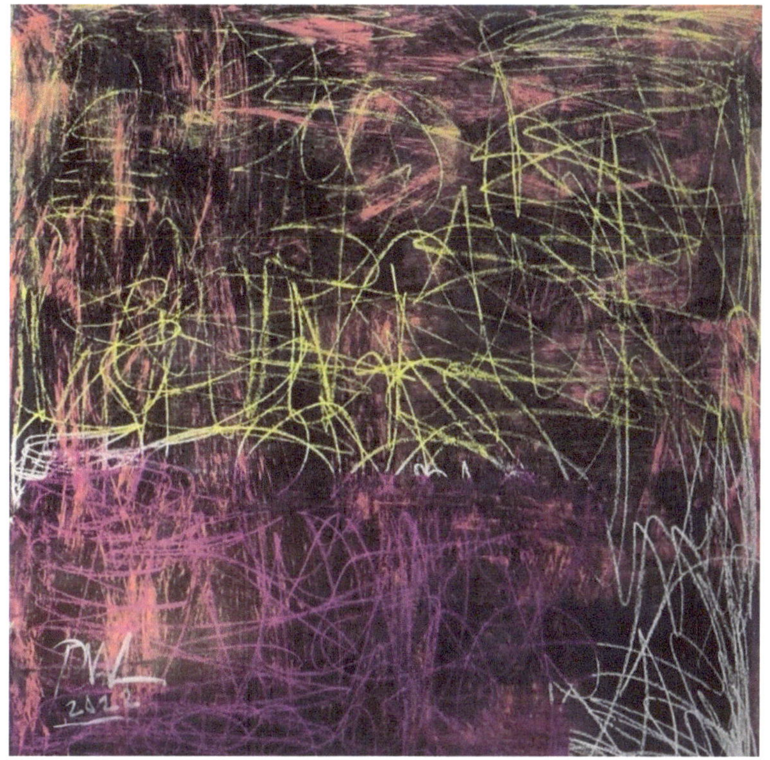

Nomadic Series #7: Bird's Nest, 2022, 4 x 4 ft, acrylic on wood.

Ram Martinez

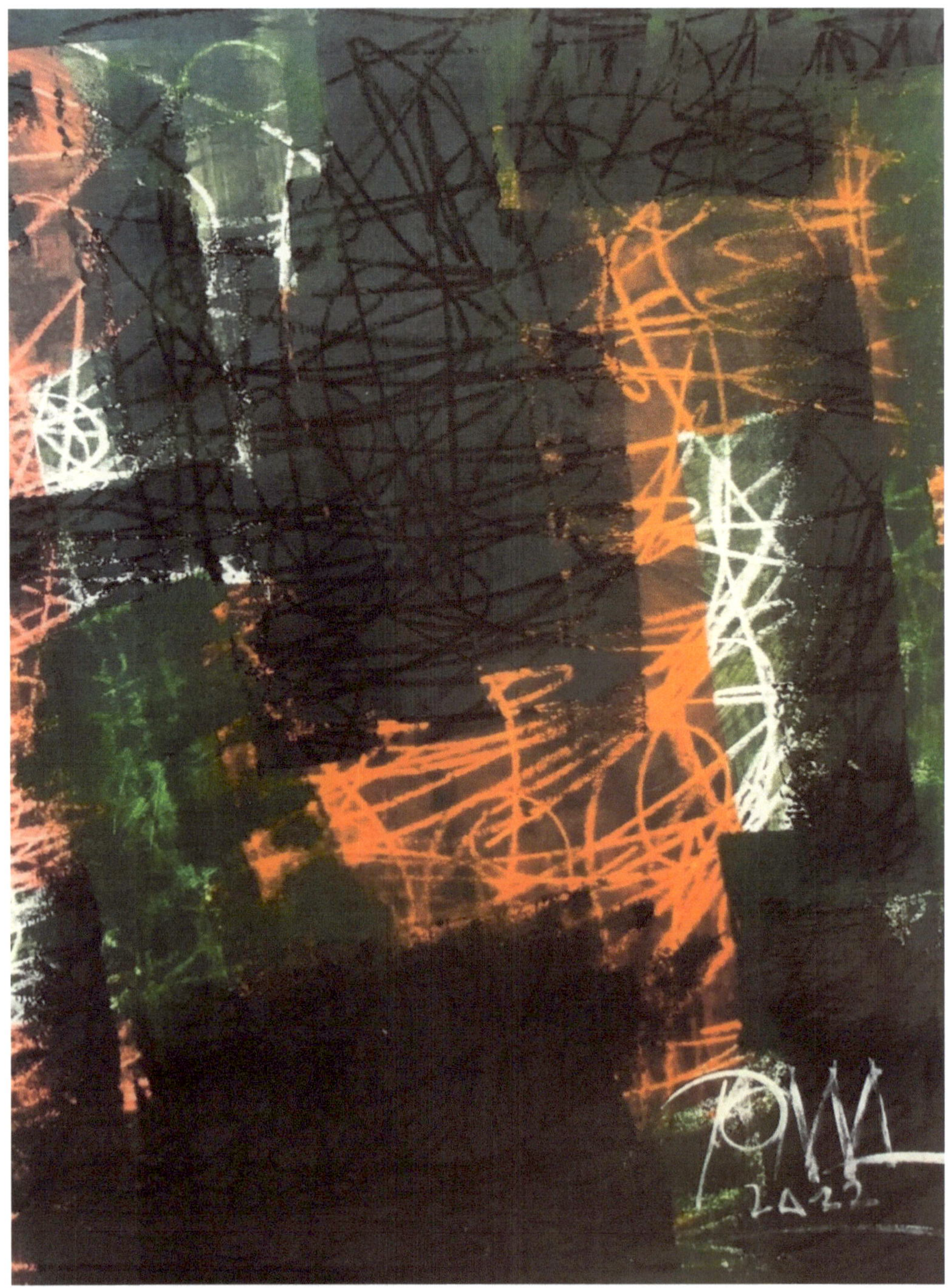

Nomadic Series #3: Moonlight Serenade, 2022, 4 x 8 ft, acrylic on wood.

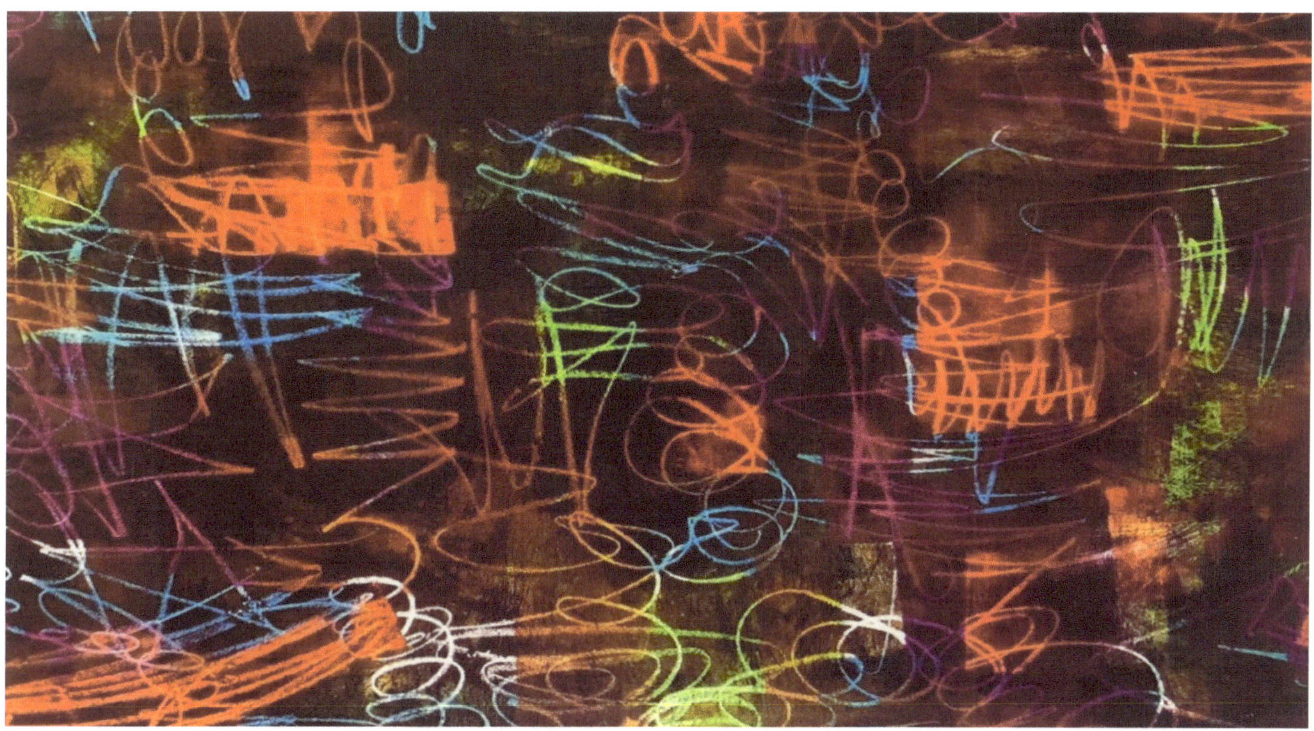

Nomadic Series #4: Midsummer's Night Dream, 2022, 4 x 8 ft, acrylic on wood.

Ram Martinez

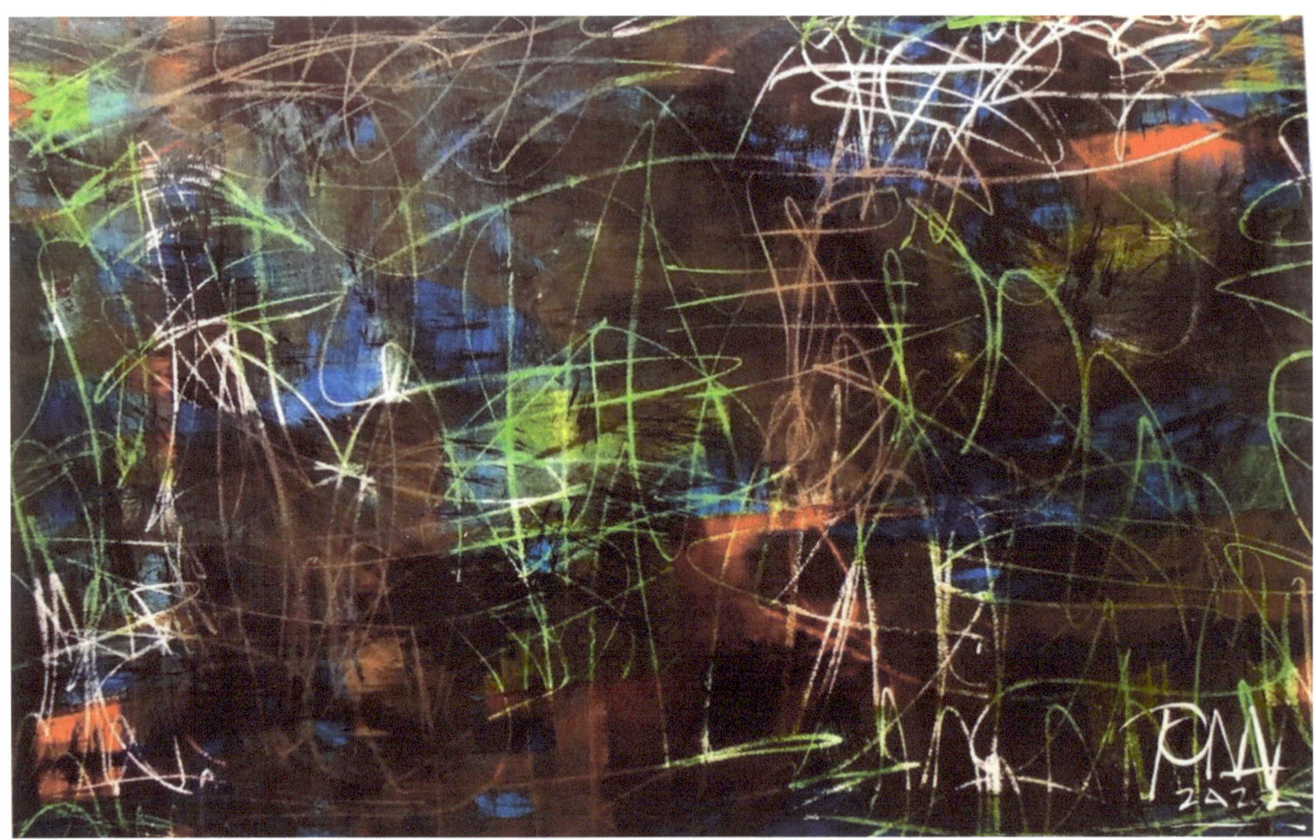

Nomadic Series #5: Noah's Ark, 2022, 4 x 8 ft, acrylic on wood.

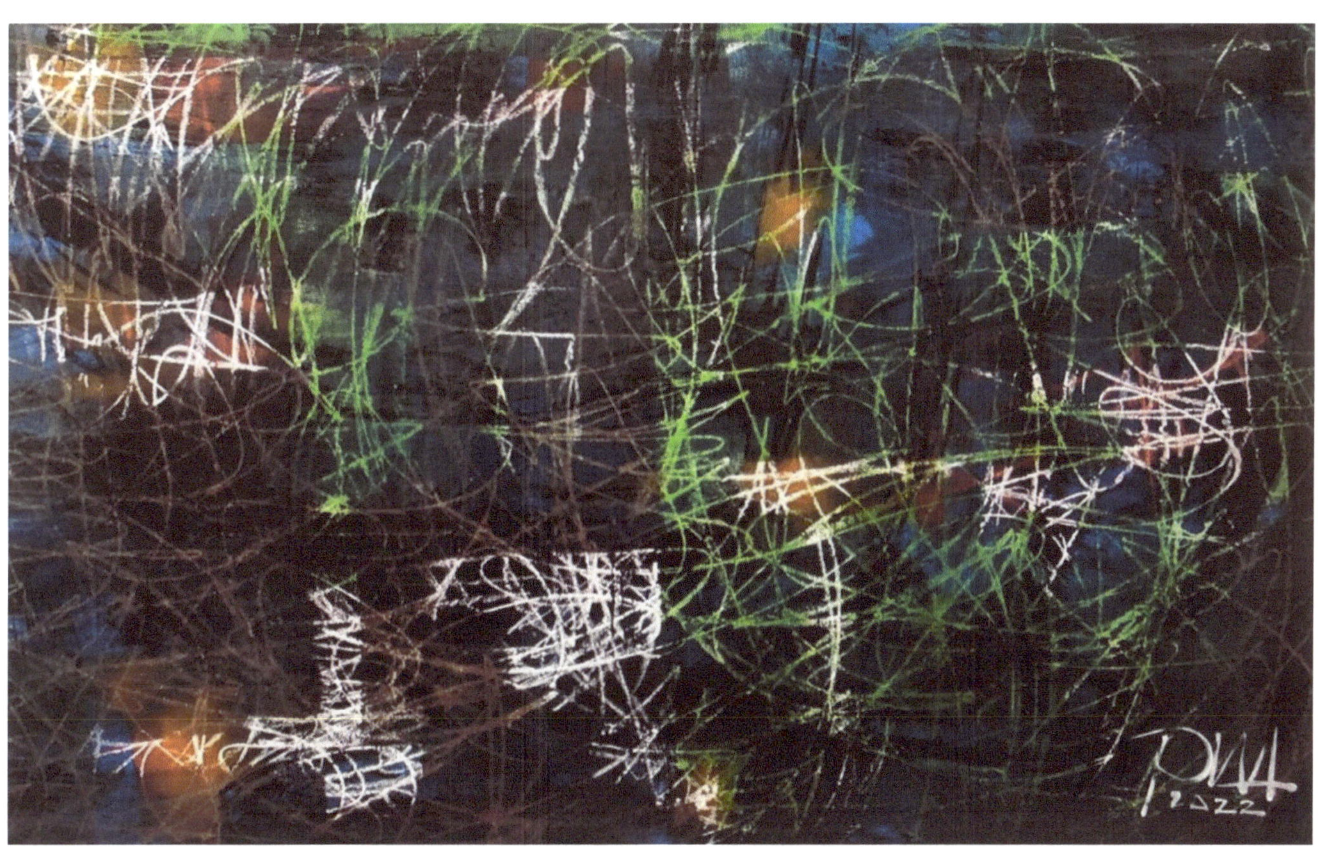

Nomadic Series #6: Harbour Lights, 2022, 4 x 8 ft, acrylic on wood.

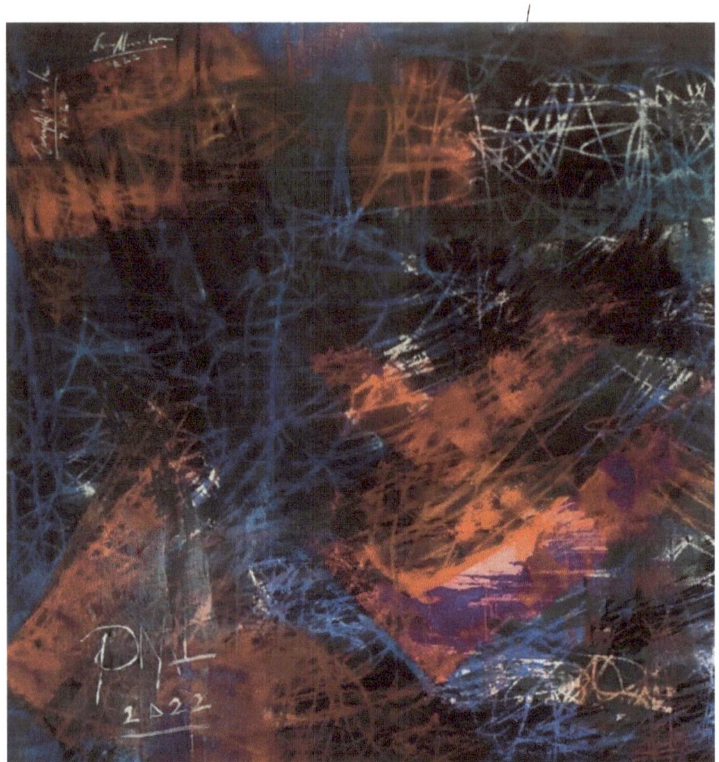

Odyssey 2022A, 4 x 4 ft, acrylic acrylic on wood.

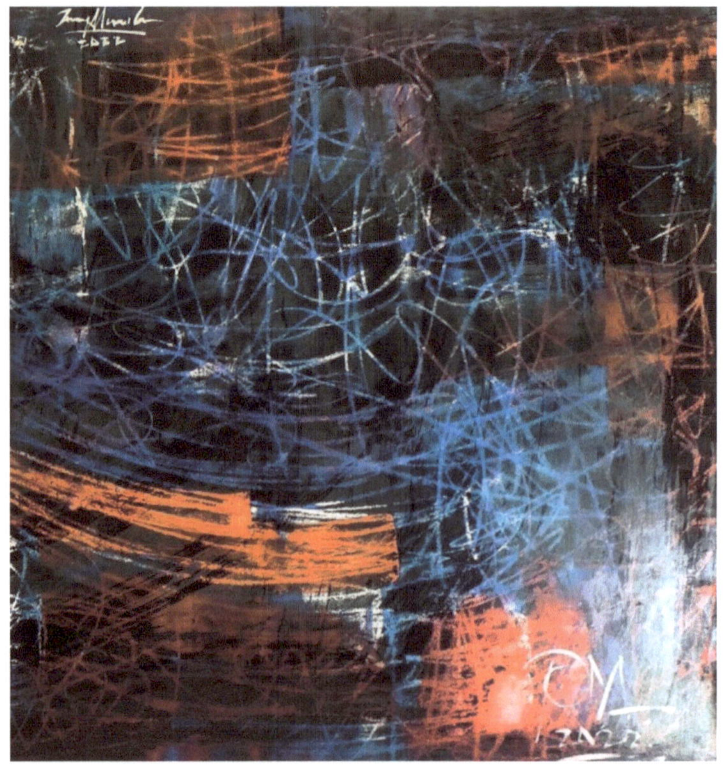

Odyssey 2022B, 4 x 4 ft, acrylic on wood.

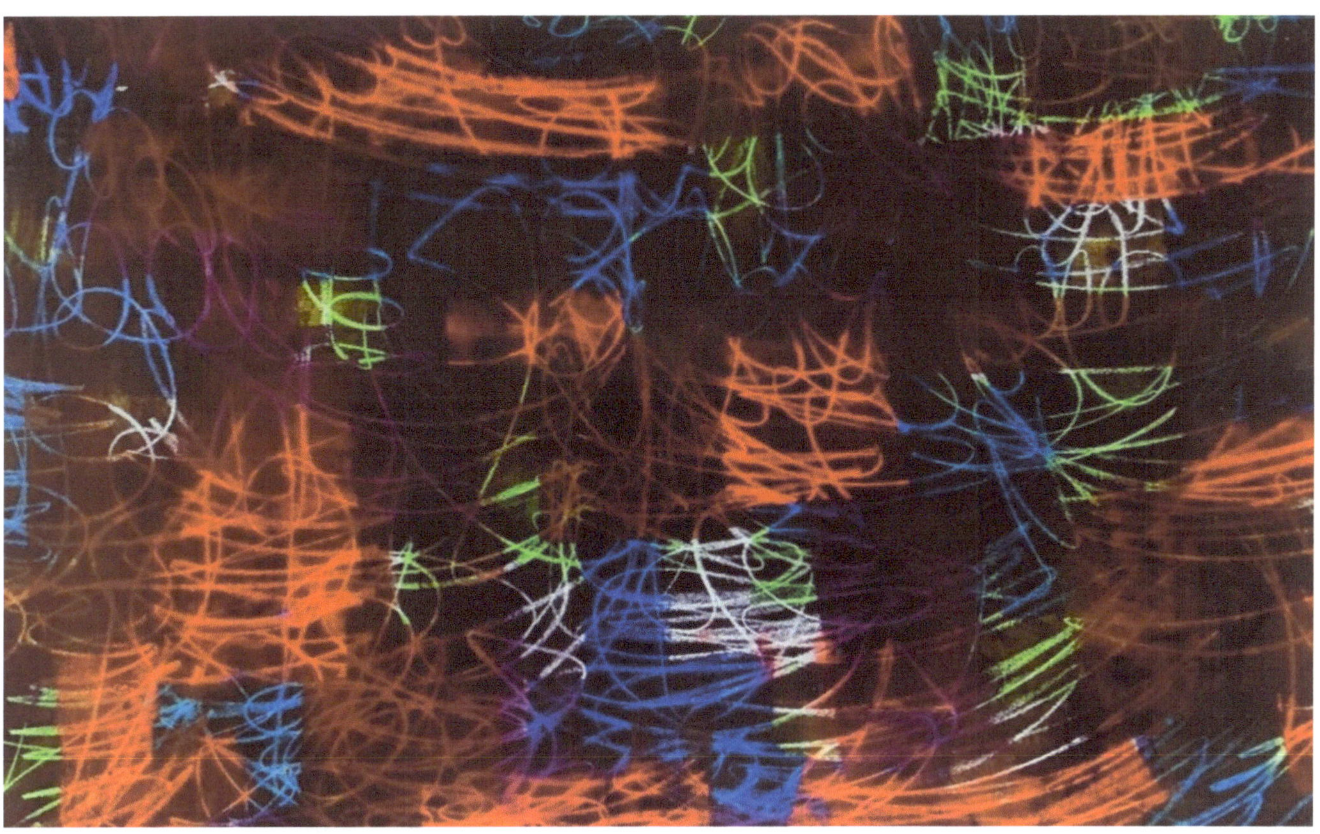

Nomadic Series #8: Fantasy, 2022, 4 x 8 ft, acrylic on wood.

AN ALCOSEBA PENTIMENTO

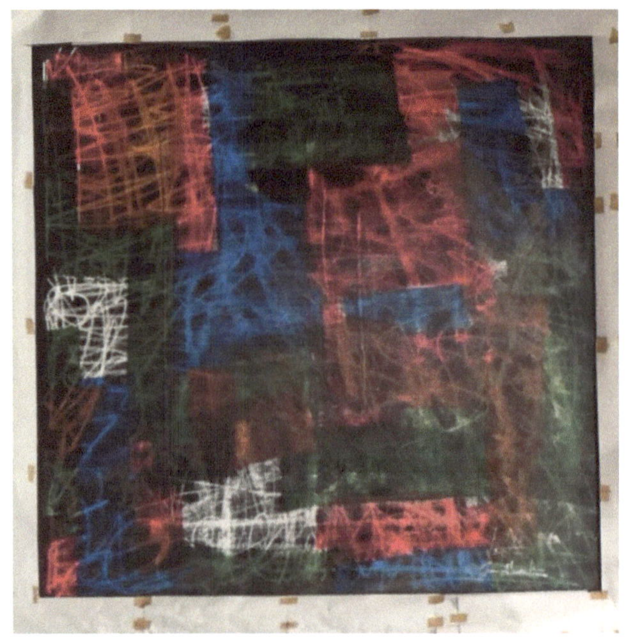

Sperma Canvas, 4 x 4 ft.

Meandering of Badjaos 2024.

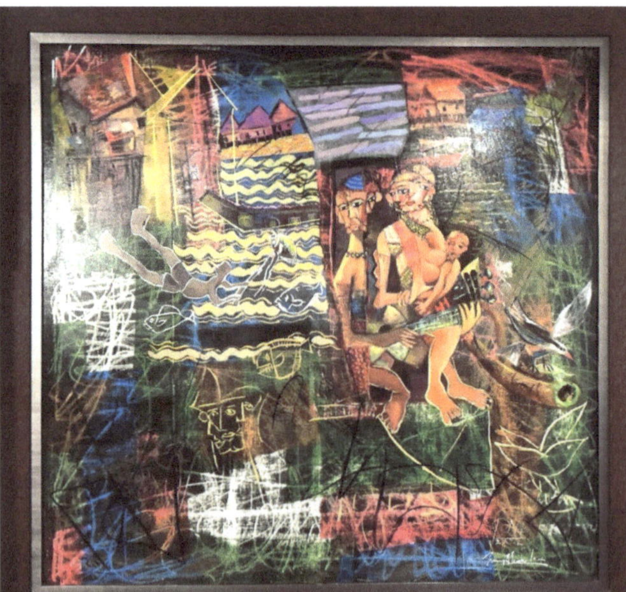

The remnants of the canvas started in 2022 above provide insight into the artist's process, revealing the evolution of the composition over time (Meandering of Badjaos 2024). Observe underlying layers and the depth and complexity to the finished artwork in the second picture below the first which offers viewers a glimpse into the artist's creative journey.

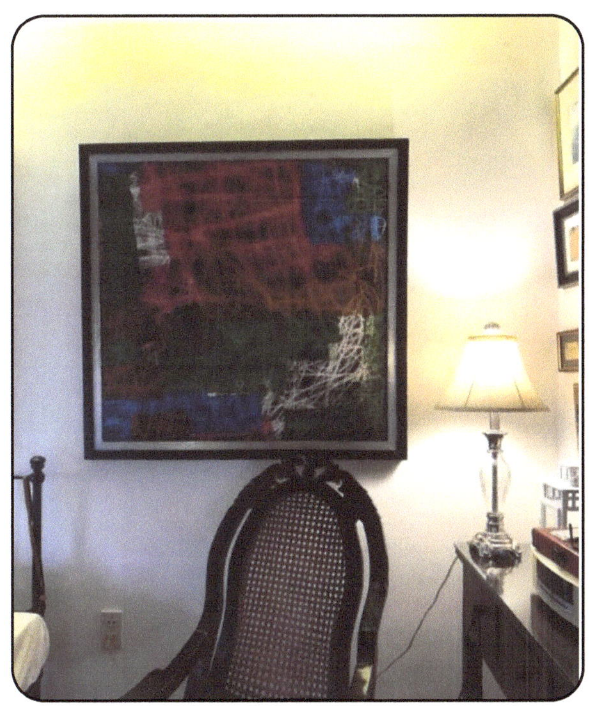

THE *Meandering of the Badjaos 2024* perfectly captures his many varied forays into his artistic discoveries and rediscoveries. To appreciate Tony's works viewers must scrutinized the objects- and or characters in a more discerning manner as if they were sight seers encountering a different group of people within the very same environment.

His depiction of humans, are those of characters that are uniquely distinct separated and defined by culture, different from one island to the next yet riding the very same ebbs and flows of survival.

Tony's lines similarly swirl across the entire canvas, inviting questions akin to Jackson Pollack's 'drip technique' of pouring paint straight from a can or along a stick onto a horizontally lying canvas.

How does one achieve this effect with a variety of colors but maintain continuity?

His never-ending lines form geometric shapes in a continuous sequence. The sight of Badjaos on the streets, begging for loose change or swimming with babies tucked to their waists to catch coins tossed into the sea, is truly mesmerizing.

The painting was created in 2022 and was finished in the early part of 2024. The 2 years belied by the detailed intricate details and its large but not massive scale. It actually took the blending and marriage of both the 3-faces and the sperma technique to partially complete the painting almost as a form of repentance in acknowledgement of a previously unseen flaw in the original work. Tony's humility and almost obsessive drive as an artist are best encapsulated in the strong expressive narrative of this particular art work.

The Meandering of the Badjaos 2024 may as well be a shadow of Tony's story.

SPERMA: A GLIMPSE INTO THE TECHNIQUE

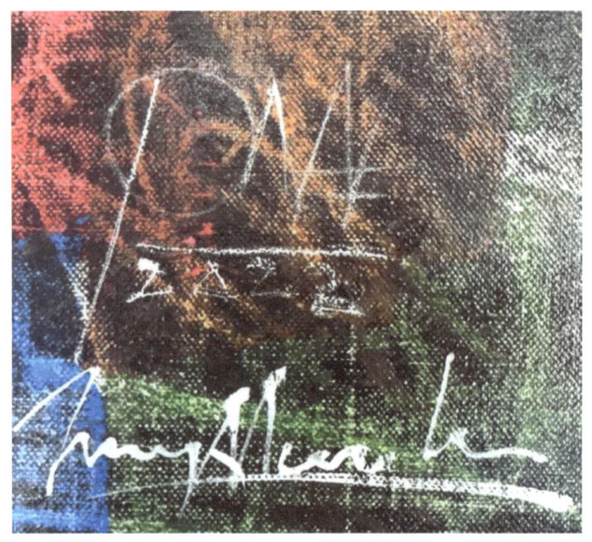

Detail of Alcoseba's signature, photo c. 2024.

THE question now is, how is this seemingly simple picture of swirling colors and forms achieved-Symphonic abstraction as Tony refers to is actually a result of a technique he has subtly employed. Initially, Tony was hesitant to reveal his technique. He believed that if his method were shared, many would experiment with it and potentially surpass his version. However, inspired by the way Jackson Pollock's drip technique was influenced by Janet Sobel, Tony eventually decided to share his process with the world in the hope of inspiring others.

At first glance, one might dismiss Tony's technique as resembling a child's scribbling or aimless doodling. However, as easy symphonic abstraction might look, one will be forced to ask what kind of brush was used or simply how it was achieved. Certainly, it is not easy to doodle with a brush around a 4ft x 4ft canvas, as in the case of *Symphonic Rhapsody* 2022. On a lawanit panel with a dimension of 4ft x 8ft, as in the case of *Odyssey 2022* and again in the *Meandering of Badjaos 2024*, it might be easier, but what exact kind of brush could create perfect connected lines, circles, and continuous patterns in different colors? How is it even possible for lines to continue to swirl into different colors? Achieving this effect on canvas or on board is far from simple. We have to remember that technique is how the artists uses and manipulates his materials to express his ideas or feelings. Tony was initially hesitant to share and eventually he opened up.

Tony begins with a blank canvas, painting it with a plain white base. Over this, he applies colors of his choice. Then, he spreads and rubs paraffin wax across the entire canvas, swirling it vigorously. This step is crucial, as the wax creates a "plastic flow," allowing the paint to move fluidly without deforming elastically in response to his forceful swirling. This method allows the paint to flow in a manner that feels almost like a sublimation of matter, where solids become elastic enough to create the desired effect. The flow and deformation properties of an acrylic paint can be referred to in terms of its Rheology.[2]

When Tony applies darker colors, the swirling lines emerge as if by magic. This phenomenon, reminiscent of the Greek philosopher Heraclitus' concept of *"panta rei"* (everything flows), illustrates that given enough time, everything will indeed flow. The final result is a series of interconnected lines, joined seamlessly yet distinguished by different colors, creating a continuous swirling effect that captivates the viewer.

---

[2]   Rheology is crucial in understanding the mechanical behavior of a wide range of substances, including acrylic which are composed of polymers and copolymers in which the major monomerics belong to ester-acrylates and methacrylates families. Acrylic paint falls under the substances studied in rheology. Painting acrylic over wax is generally not recommended. Sanding after the application of the wax made the acrylic paint adhere properly.

THE CAT SERIES: ONE GIANT STEP

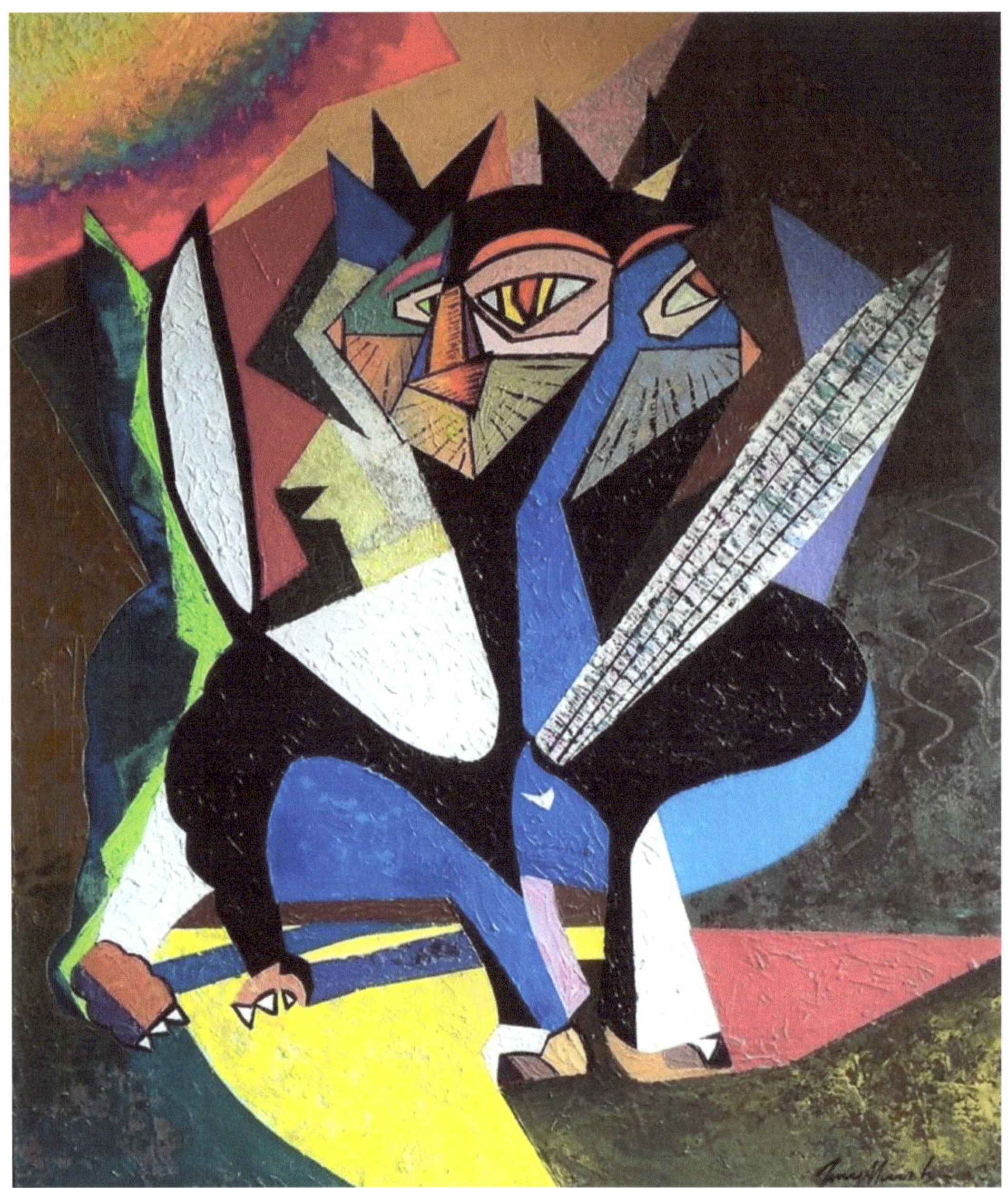

El Gato 1986, 22 x 30 in, acrylic on canvas (also title page).

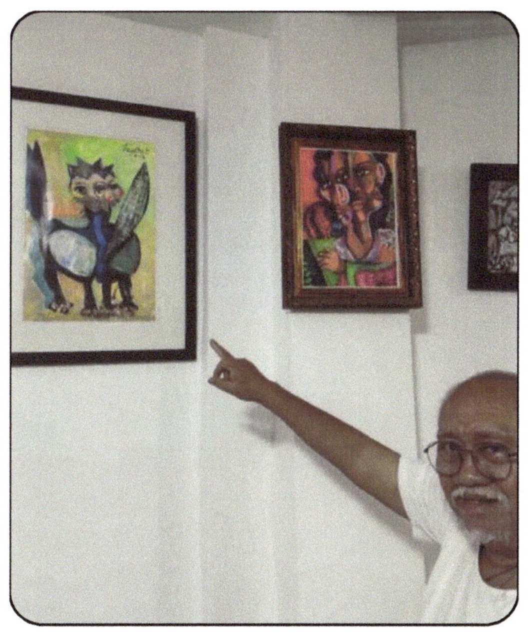

EL GATO *1986* was Tony's one giant step. El Gato marked a significant turning point in Tony's artistic journey. It was during this period that Tony began to delve into the depths of ideas that had long been brewing within his creative mind, initially sparked by his formative experiences in the field of Architecture. However, despite the burgeoning inspiration, Tony found himself facing a challenging transition as he navigated the complexities of fully embracing these new concepts.

Throughout the late 1980s and into the early 2000s, spanning the tumultuous landscape of the Asian financial crisis and beyond, Tony's artistic endeavors struggled to find solid ground. His departure from the familiar realms of representational art left many of his loyal Cebuano patrons and buyers bewildered and disconnected. Accustomed to the vibrant hues of his watercolors and the tangible narratives of his oil paintings, they grappled to reconcile with Tony's newfound abstract style, questioning the very essence of his signature artistic expression. Here's an extracted email message of Tony to a patron from Manila.

"Transitions/shifts are never easy because comparisons are bound to happen - like how come a painting of a woman does not really look like a woman but appears like a figure dissolving in the joys of summer (realism to impressionism).

Or in your words, fineness, simplicity and life as different in my recent works when compared to my earlier ones…

Transitions/shifts, too, endanger the relationship between artist and viewer. Because the relationship has been based on something "secure" in the past, anything new would be viewed with suspicion.

And, I think this is where, as in my experience, artists and viewers need to dialogue. The artist "confessing" about his creative cloud; the viewer articulating what he sees in the latest works of an artist as products of this creative cloud.

You said it well yourself. That concept is on the part of the artist but appreciation is on the viewer."

In the midst of these artistic trials and tribulations, Tony found himself confronted with the harsh realities of the commercial art world. A contract with CAP, a prominent Philippine insurance company, ended in turmoil amidst the financial upheaval of 1997.

Despite purportedly selling only one painting, Tony found himself embroiled in a legal dispute over the remaining balance, a testament to the challenges inherent in navigating the intricacies of the art market. The organizers demanded payment for the said remaining balance, which Tony disputed in court and won.

Artists themselves evolve. Their style, technique, and thematic focus often change throughout their careers as they experiment, learn, and grow. While art may often be spontaneous in its creation, it is also shaped by an ongoing process of change and development.

Amidst these setbacks, Tony remained steadfast in his commitment to his craft, recognizing the gradual and often arduous process of creating art grounded solely in abstract principles.

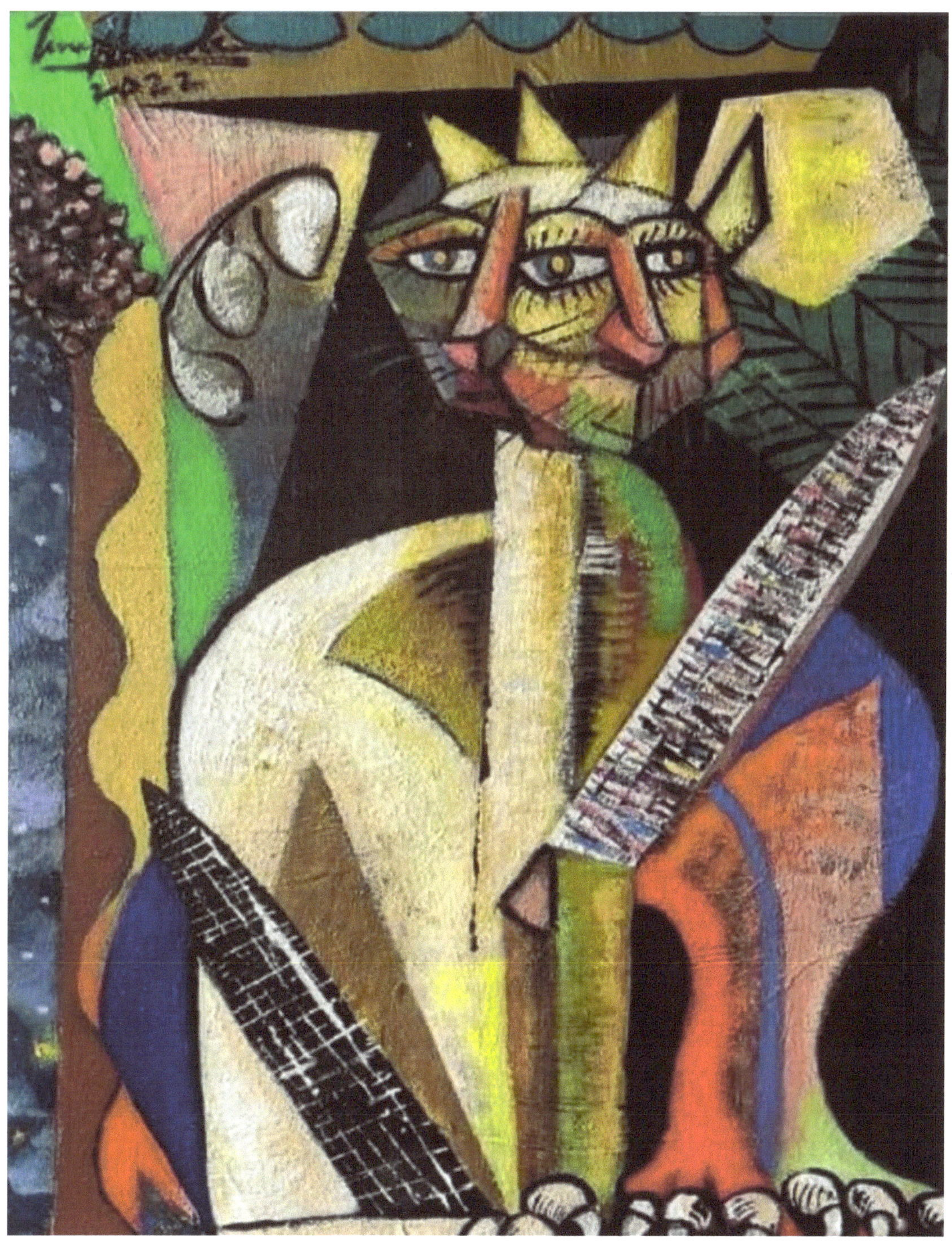

Prince of Night 2023 , 22 x 30 in, acrylic on arches paper, in private collection.

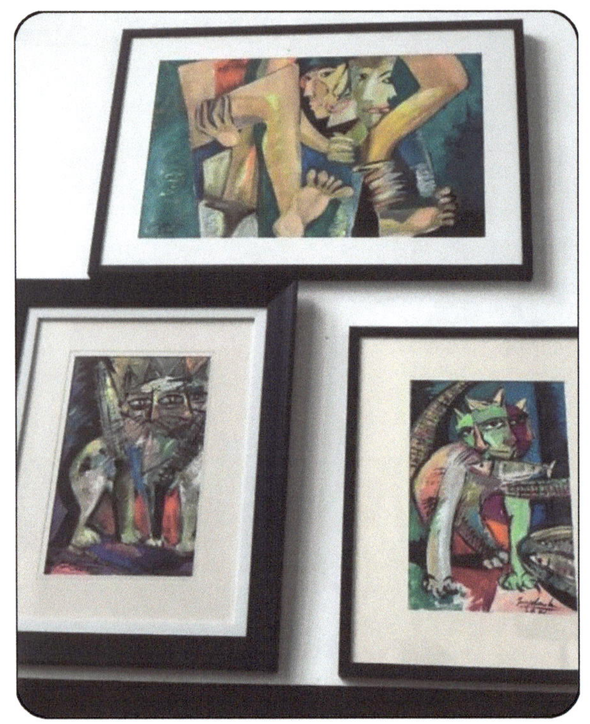

LET us get back to the subject of cats. *El Gato* in 1986 is a prominent piece from Tony's CAT series, measuring 22 x 30 inches. This painting features a stylized depiction of a cat using geometric forms and a vibrant, contrasting color palette. The cat is portrayed in a symmetrical pose, allowing viewers to see both sides of its body, but with a twist: its tail, a signature element in Tony's work, like most of the cat series, is re-positioned in front of its back, adding a unique dimension to the composition. There are other paintings in this series but for purposes of brevity, let us dissect this particular cat.

The composition is structured around a central axis of symmetry, with the cat's body divided into mirrored halves. The original painting also had a custom-made frame made of mirrors. If that helps complete a picture. The geometric forms—triangles, squares, and circles—are meticulously arranged to construct the cat's outline and internal features.

The re-positioned tail breaks the symmetry slightly, drawing attention to Tony's playful manipulation of traditional forms. This deliberate disruption invites viewers to reconsider the boundaries of symmetry and asymmetry.

Tony utilizes a bold, varied color scheme, incorporating bright reds, deep blues, vibrant yellows, and stark blacks. These colors are strategically placed to create a sense of depth and movement within the rigid geometric framework. The juxtaposition of warm and cool tones not only defines the cat's form but also creates an optical illusion, suggesting multiple images within the primary subject. This interplay of colors encourages viewers to see beyond the cat which evokes different interpretations and forms hidden within the abstraction.

The painting features smooth, precise brushwork that enhances the clarity of the geometric shapes. The texture is generally flat, emphasizes the abstract nature of the work. However, subtle variations in the application of paint add a tactile quality to certain areas, giving the composition a sense of dynamism. The medium was definitely acrylic. This technique helps to soften the rigid geometry and makes the forms appear more fluid and interconnected.

Now let us also look into the themes. In *El Gato* 1986 Tony certainly explores themes of perception, identity, and transformation. The symmetrical depiction of the cat, a familiar and beloved subject, invites viewers to examine the concept of duality and reflection. The re-positioned tail, a trademark of Tony's style, symbolizes a break from conventional representations and challenges viewers to see beyond the obvious. The use of geometric forms as a means of reduction underscores the idea that simplicity can reveal complexity and suggests that even the most straightforward shapes can contain multitudes.

This particular painting and much of the cat series conjure a sense of curiosity and wonder. The vibrant colors and geometric precision create an engaging visual experience, while the abstracted form of the cat invites personal interpretation and reflection. The slight asymmetry introduced by the tail adds an element of surprise, prompting viewers to explore the artwork more deeply and to uncover the hidden images suggested by the interplay of shapes and colors.

Tony has the ability to blend abstraction with recognizable forms. The use of geometric shapes to depict the cat is both innovative and visually striking and demonstrates a keen understanding of how reduction can enhance complexity. The bold color choices and the careful positioning of the tail showcase Tony's playful yet thoughtful approach to art. While the abstraction might be challenging for some viewers who prefer more representational art, the painting's strength lies in its ability to engage and provoke thought through its simplicity and depth. The balance between symmetry and deliberate disruption adds a dynamic quality to the piece, making it a standout work in Tony's paintings.

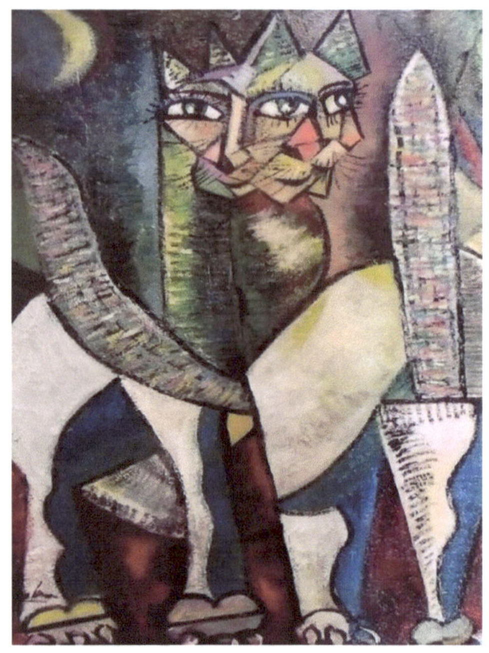

Cat Series #1, 2022, 20 x 28 in acrylic on board.

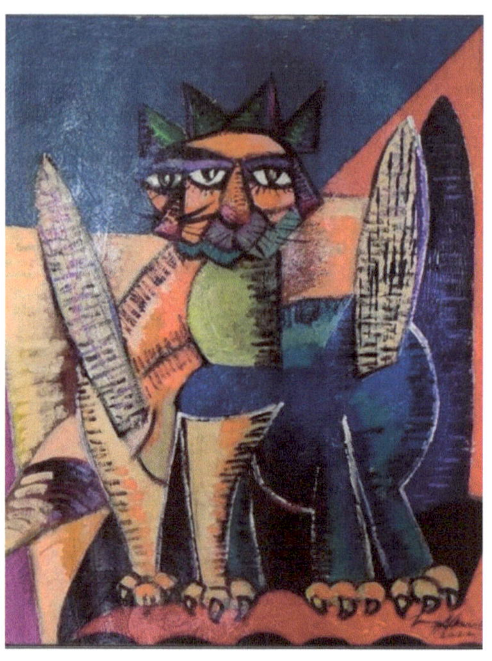

Cat Series #2, 2023 20 x 30 in acrylic on board.

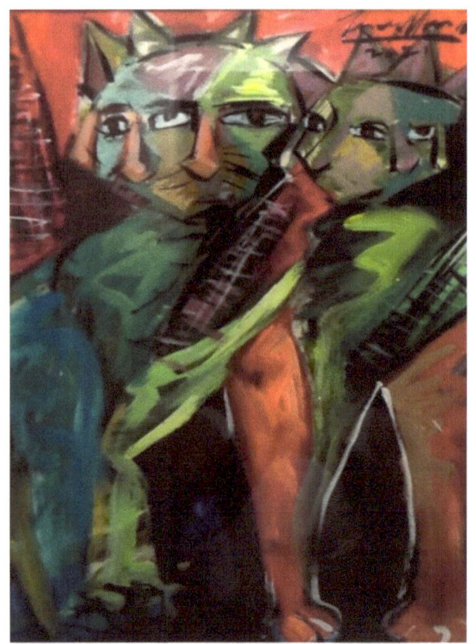

Cat Series #3, 12 x 18 in acrylic on board.

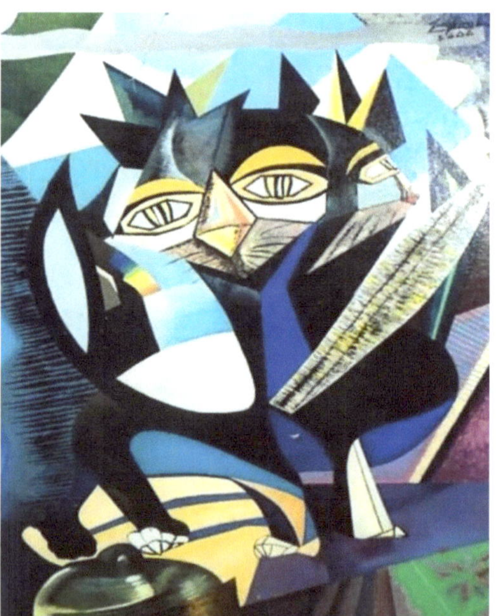

Cat Series #4, 8 x 20 in, acrylic on board, collection of John Paul Uy.

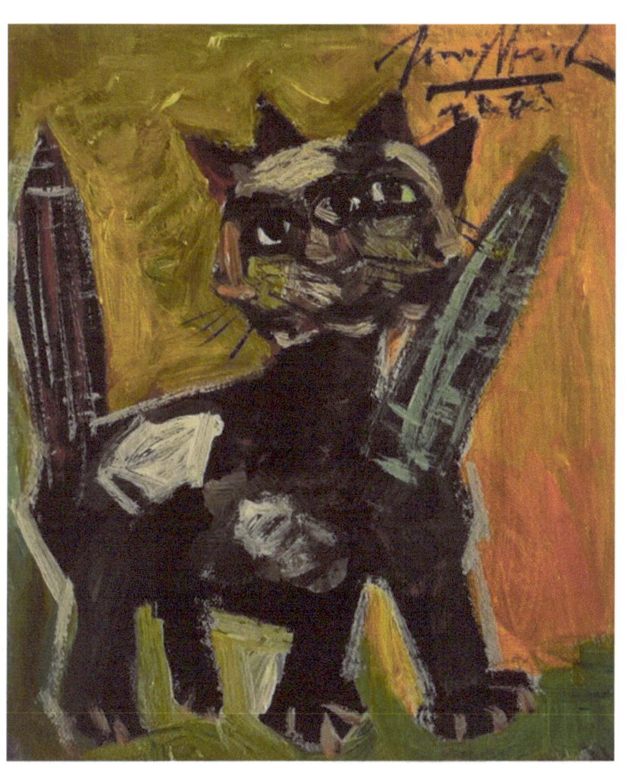

Cat Series #5, 2020, 12 x 16 in, acrylic on canvas.

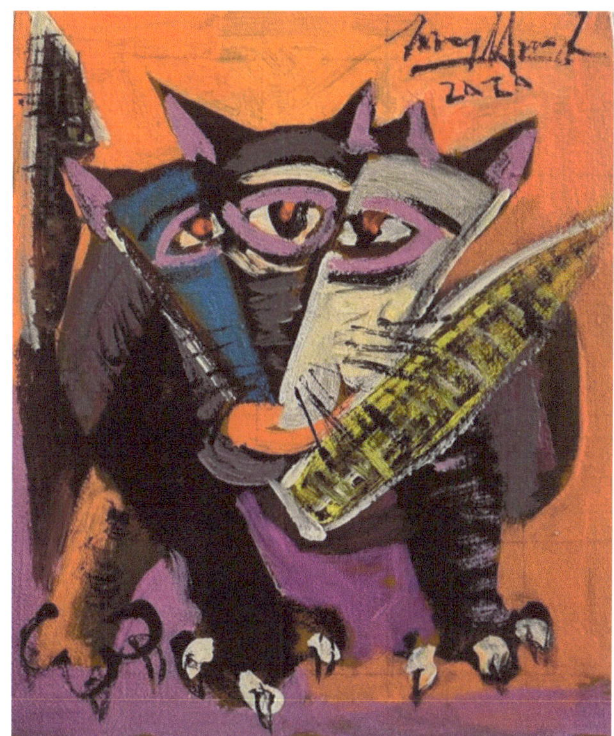

Cat Series #6, 2020, 10 x 12 in, acrylic on canvas.

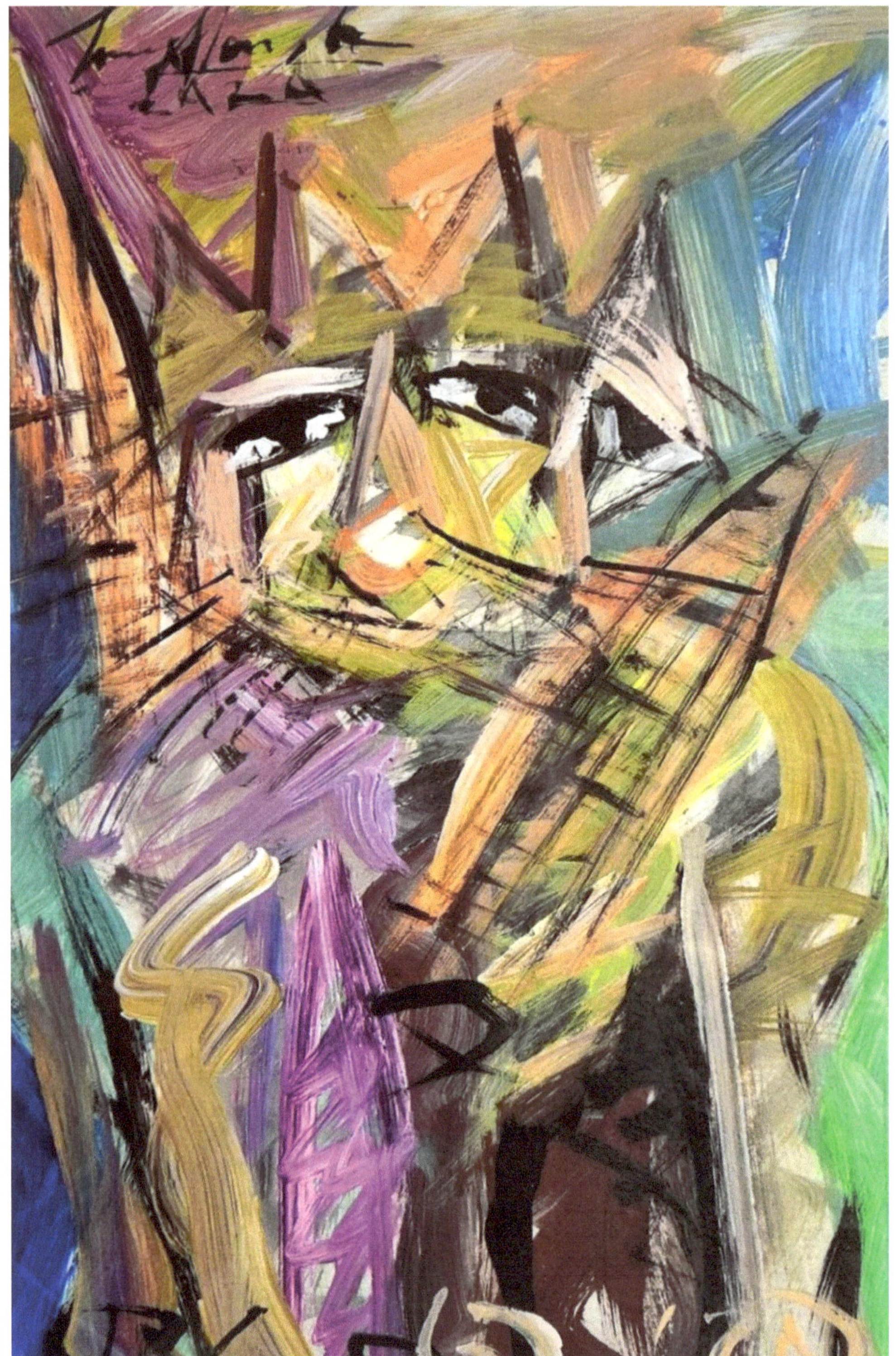

Cat Series #7, 2020, 10.5 x 17.5 in, acrylic on board, collection of
Dr. Richard Myles Montesclaros.

THE TARTANILLA SERIES

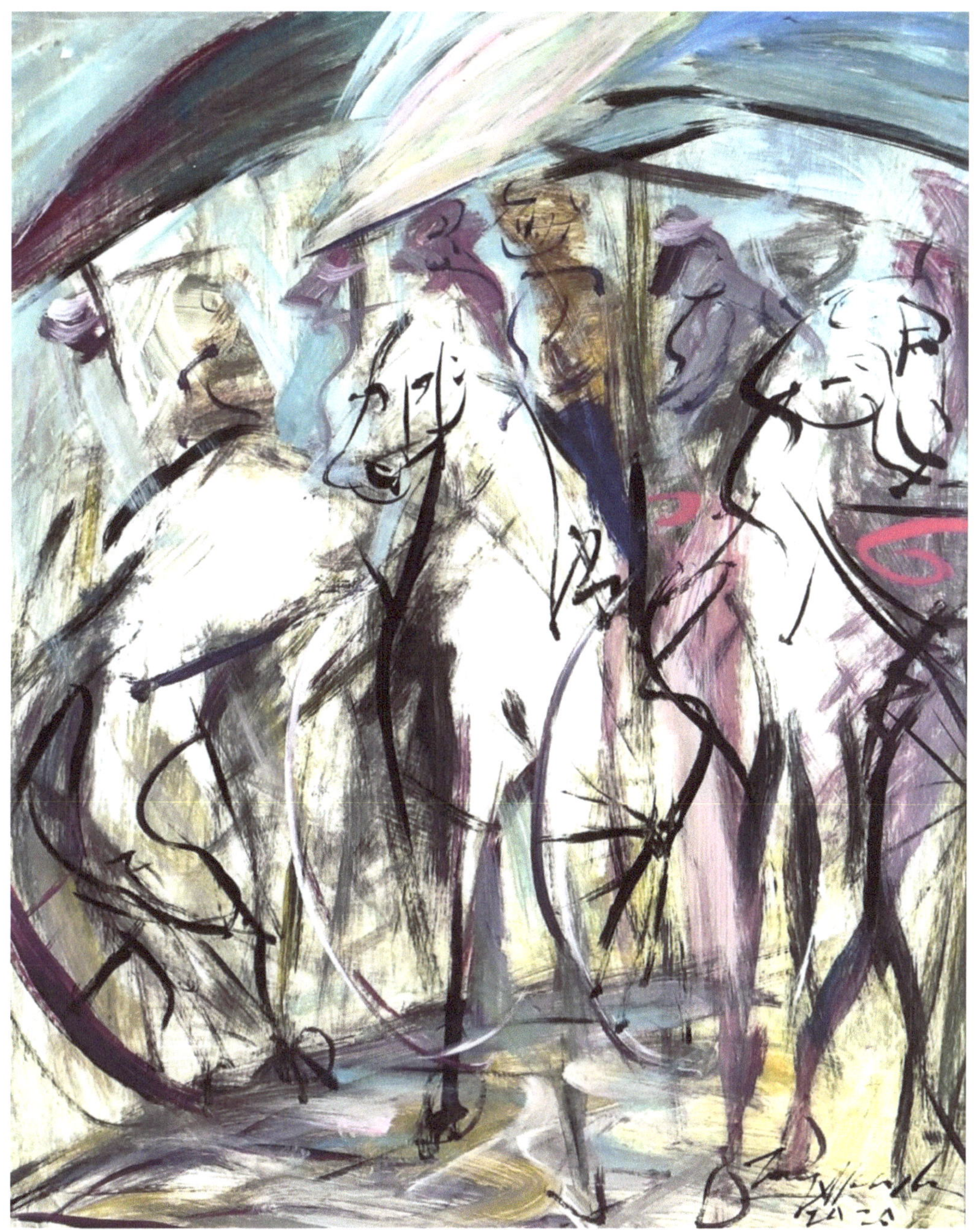

Tartanilla Series #1, 2020 20 x 30 in, acrylic on board.

Ram Martinez

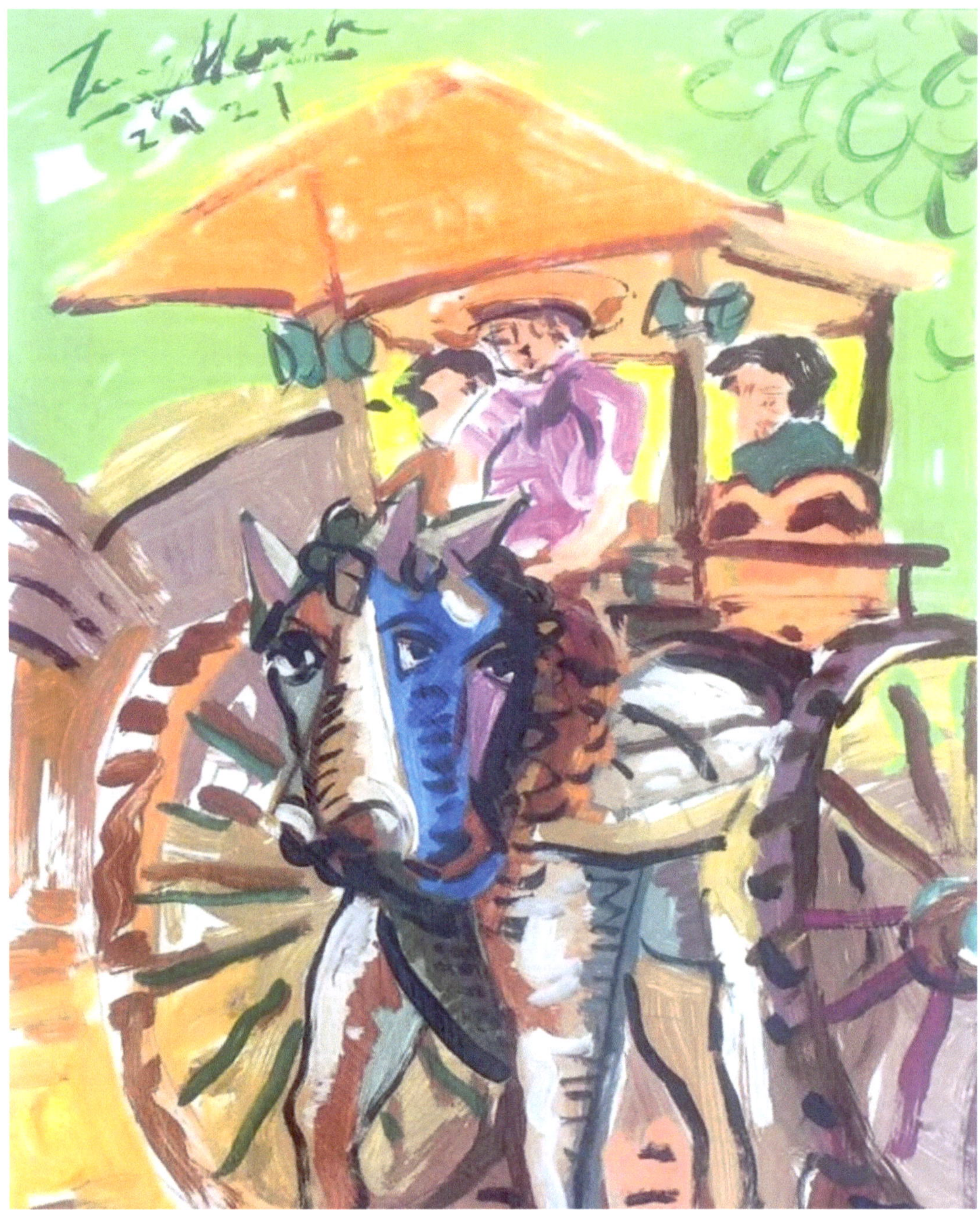

Tartanilla Series #2, 2021, 15 x 20 in, acrylic on board.

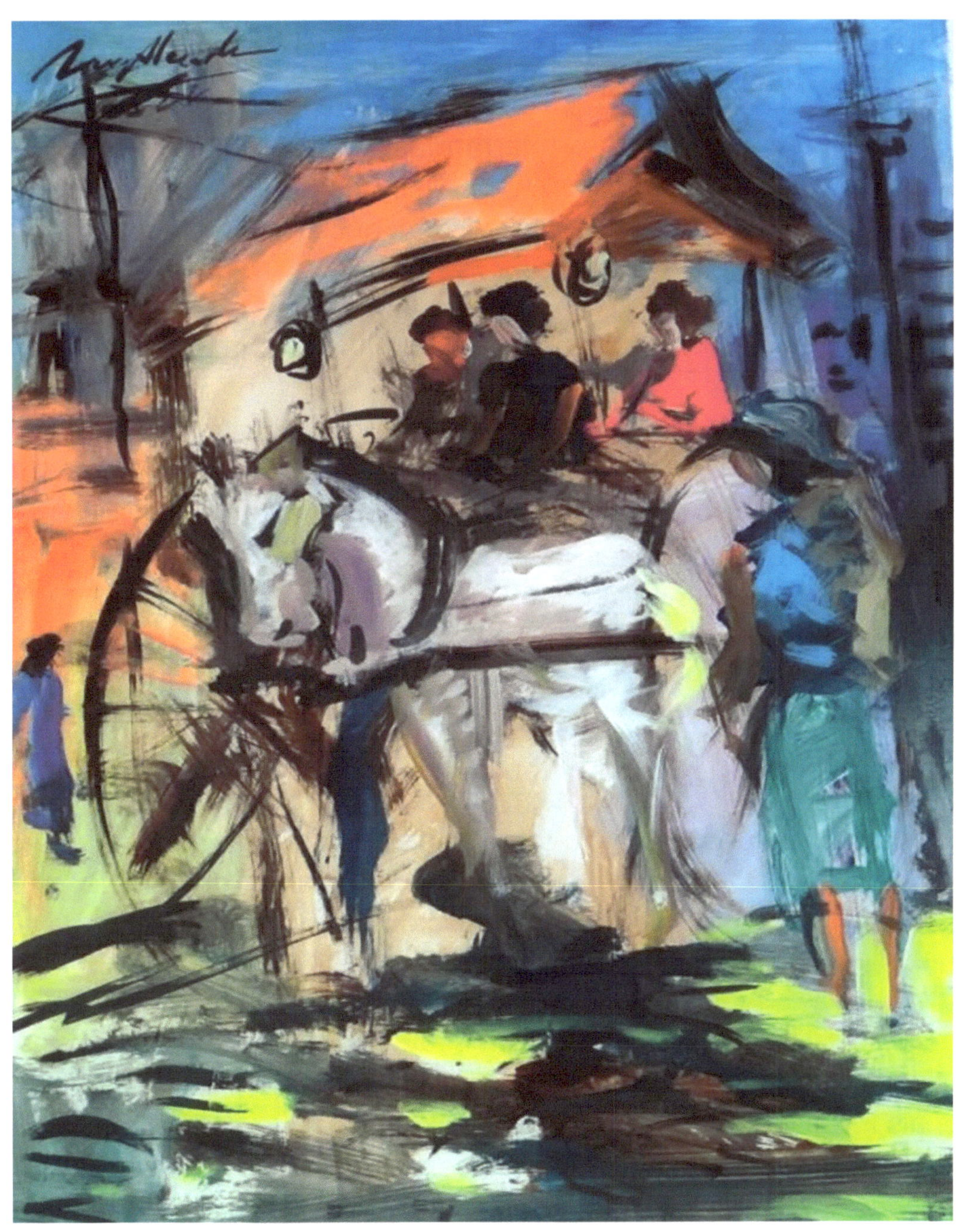

Tartanilla Series #3, 2022, 2 x 3 ft, acrylic on board, collection of Rebecca A. Martinez.

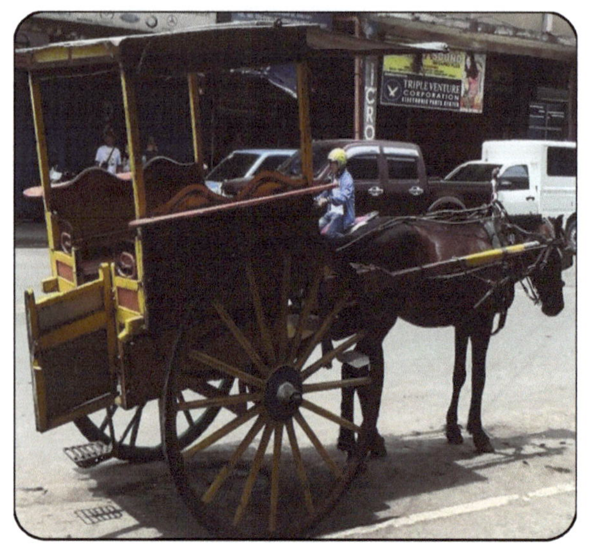

TONY grew up near Sanciangko Street and Jones Avenue, steeped in the nostalgic charm of horse-drawn *tartanillas* which serves as a poignant reminder of the passage of time and ever-evolving landscape of his beloved city. In the 1960s, all the way through the late 1980s, tartanillas traversed the streets of Sanciangko, where his grandfather, Jose (Peping) Trinidad Alcoseba, once resided. Today, *tartanillas*[3] are merely memories from a far-gone era. These horse-drawn carriages are now confined to some obscure streets with less traffic.

The echoes of Jose Tr. Alcoseba, a UST fine arts graduate and a founding member of the Cebu Arts Association resonate deeply within Tony's own artistic journey. His grandfather's legacy has instilled in Tony a profound sense of duty as depicted in the *Fiesta* and *Tartanilla series* as well as in the *Harvest 2016*. These are pictures that tell stories of Filipino life and which contribute perhaps as an apt background to the cultural heritage of his community.

In his quest to capture the essence of Cebu and showcase paintings that embody a distinctively Filipino identity, Tony's artistic vision finds resonance with the pioneering spirit of Wassily Kandinsky, whose seminal work "Concerning the Spiritual in Art" challenged the conventions of artistic expression and sought to evoke a deeper, more profound connection to the spiritual realm. Like Kandinsky, Tony aspires to transcend the boundaries of mere representation and delve into the realm of the abstract to uncover the hidden truths and spiritual dimensions of his subject matter.

In this pursuit of artistic enlightenment, Tony's journey mirrors the transformative ethos of Kandinsky's philosophy, as he endeavors to infuse his paintings with the soulful essence of his Filipino heritage. Through his evocative imagery and visionary insights, Tony invites viewers to embark on a transcendent journey of discovery, where the boundaries between the physical and the metaphysical dissolve, and the true essence of Filipino identity is revealed in all its vibrant splendor.

---

[3]   Tartanilla Series: Unfortunately unearthing and or obtaining photographs of paintings from this series proved to be a challenging endeavor as well. Most paintings from these series are in private collections.

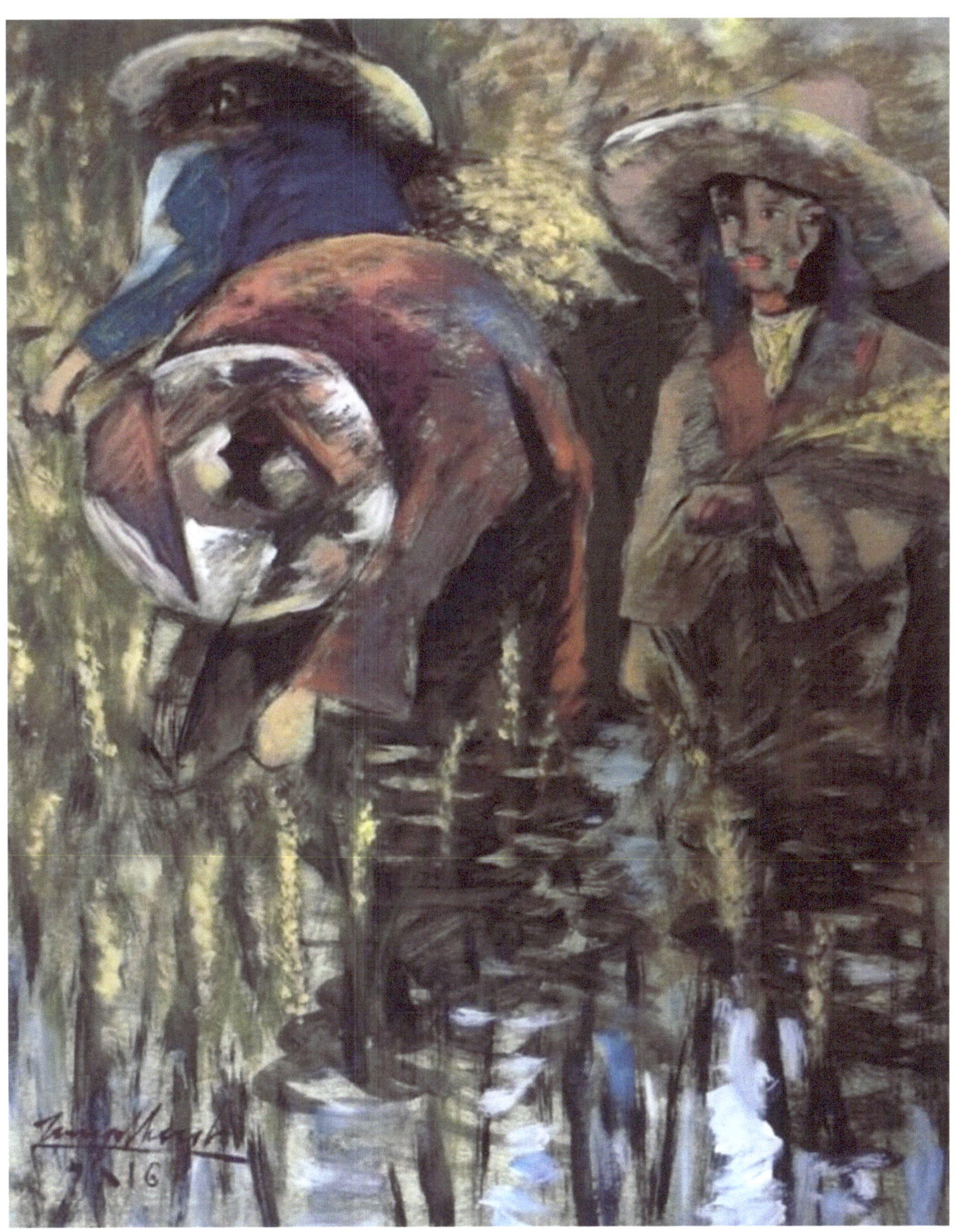

The Harvest, 2016, 20 x 30 in, acrylic on board.

CEBUANO MODERNISM: A UNIQUELY CEBUANO JOURNEY TOWARDS MODERNISM IN ART

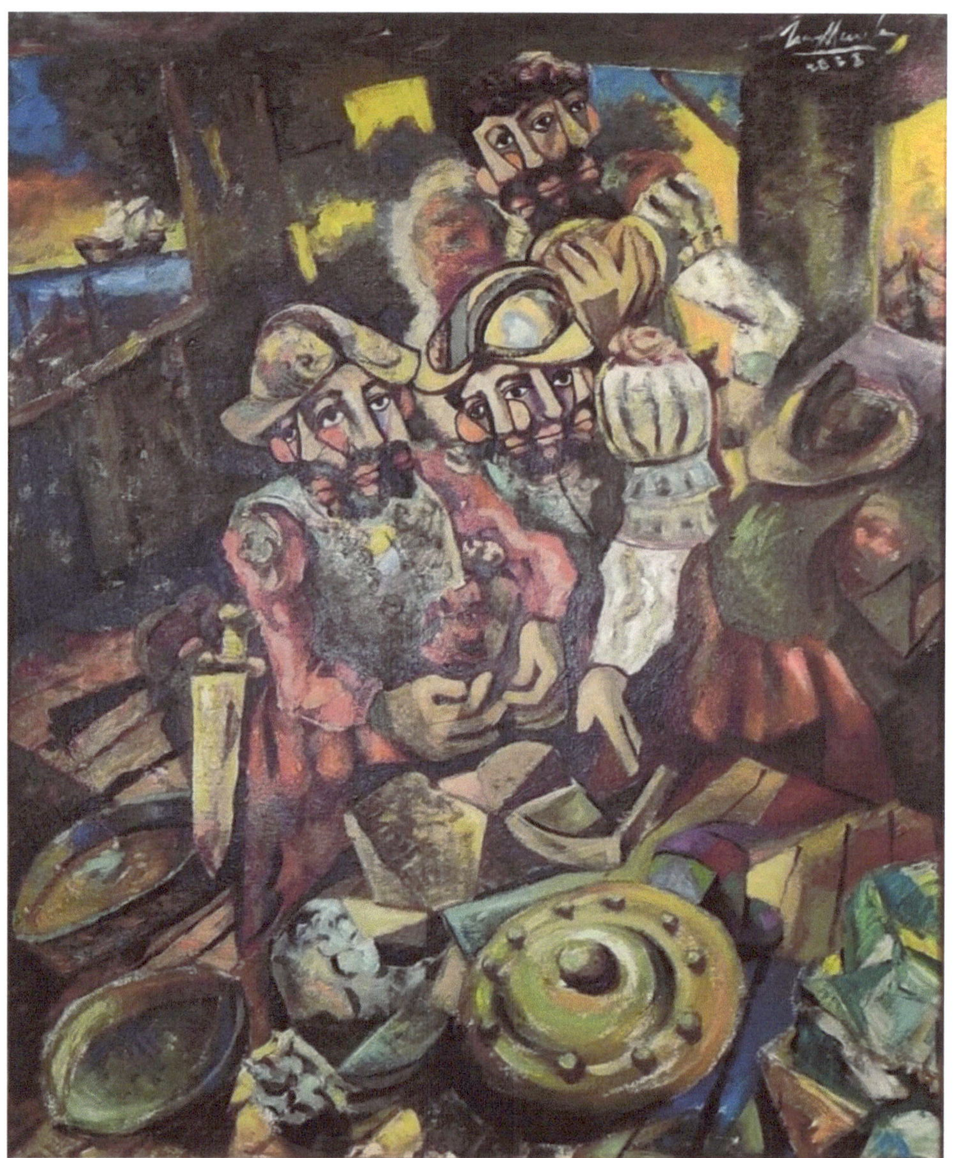

Finding the Child Jesus, 2022, 2 x 4 ft, acrylic on canvas.

IT is nearly impossible to discuss Tony's journey towards modernism without considering his past experiences. It must be noted that Tony is not alone in his journey towards modernism. He once mentioned that his training and exposure were rooted in Western art, thus watercolor and oil. However, it cannot be denied that his inclination towards abstractionism or modernism may also be influenced by his colonial background, although it is unclear if this influence is primarily American, as evidenced by the emergence of pop art in the country.

Let us delve deeper and dissect his approach as if conducting an anatomy lesson to acquaint ourselves with the artist's vision. His demeanor resembles that of a poet awaiting the arrival of his muse or a conductor awaiting the final cue from the composer. Who, then, is the composer?

In his works like *Nomadic Rhapsody 2022* and *Odyssey 2022*, the southern tribes of Badjaos serve as his tangible vehicle into the dizzying swirl of tides. It's worth noting that he didn't arrive at a destination; rather, the continuous swirling serves as his method not only for survival and relevance in changing times but also for interpreting the same concepts repeatedly, with no end in sight. Perhaps he hoped to attain understanding or a new interpretation through the iteration of lines and forms.

The bilateral symmetry of cats, serving as subjects in Tony's geometrical abstraction for his "3-faces" technique, represents perfect anatomy. Notice how the tail is consistently positioned almost in front, a feature absent in humans. The "3-faces" technique he now possessed poses challenges as a subject compared to cats, especially in relating it to the entirety of human anatomy.

Experimentation and innovation with forms, shapes, etc. were difficult for him as well because he remained acutely aware of his transcendent history.

It's worth mentioning that the Alcosebas of Cebu were honored as one of the 75 distinguished families during the charter day event in September 2011 which highlighted their contributions to visual arts and religious apostolate. Tony's devout Catholicism is evident in his works featuring the *Finding the Child Jesus Sto. Niño 2022*, the *Cruxificion 2018* and *San Pedro Calungsod 2012* (the second Filipino saint canonized by Benedict XVI only in 2012) reflecting his reverence for tradition and spirituality. For the saint's beatification commemoration, Tony in fact contributed 50 digitally produced San Pedro Calungsod paintings to the Archdiocese. Each painting comes with a certificate of authenticity featuring the late Ricardo Cardinal Vidal's signature.

In Tony's nomadic series, inspired by the culture of the Badjao people, he delves into a rich tapestry of traditions and customs that have endured for centuries. The Badjao, a nomadic sea-faring tribe, traverse the waters of Southeast Asia, their lives intimately intertwined with the ebb and flow of the tides. Tony's exploration of this culture serves as a profound metaphor for the human experience and reflects themes of movement, adaptability, and resilience.

Through his art, Tony captures the essence of the Badjao way of life by depicting scenes on the water with vivid detail and emotional resonance. The swirling currents of the sea become a central motif in his compositions and symbolize the constant flux of existence and the ever-changing nature of the world.

Moreover, Tony's nomadic series serves as a commentary on the broader human condition and highlights the universal themes of migration, displacement, and belonging.

In portraying the Badjao's nomadic lifestyle, he invites viewers to reflect on their own sense of identity and place in the world and prompts questions about the nature of home, community, and cultural heritage.

In Tony's exploration of modernism and abstraction, his nomadic series takes on a transformative role and serves as a canvas for his artistic experimentation and philosophical exploration. Drawing inspiration from the nomadic lifestyle of the Badjao people, Tony employs abstraction as a means of distilling complex cultural narratives into their purest visual forms.

By embracing abstraction, Tony transcends literal representation and invites viewers to engage with his work on a deeper, more intuitive level. Through the use of geometric shapes, swirling patterns, and bold colors, he captures the essence of the Badjao's nomadic existence and evokes the rhythmic ebb and flow of the sea and the ever-shifting currents of human experience.

Moreover, Tony's nomadic series serves as a reflection of the modernist ethos that challenges traditional notions of representation and narrative in art. By breaking free from conventional techniques and styles, he embraces a spirit of innovation and experimentation and pushes the boundaries of artistic expression to new heights.

In this context, abstraction becomes a powerful tool for Tony to explore the universal themes of movement, adaptation, and resilience that define the human condition. Through his bold use of form and color, he invites viewers to contemplate the deeper meanings behind his work and encourages them to see beyond the surface and engage with the underlying essence of his artistic vision.

Ultimately, Tony's nomadic series represents a bold and innovative approach to both abstraction and modernism and bridges the gap between past and present, tradition and innovation. Through his evocative imagery and philosophical insights, he challenges us to rethink our preconceptions about art and its role in shaping our understanding of the world.

Furthermore, Tony's engagement with the Badjao culture extends beyond mere representation, as he seeks to capture the essence of their spiritual beliefs and philosophical outlook. Through his art, he explores themes of inter-connectedness, harmony with nature, and the cyclical rhythms of life and death by inviting viewers to contemplate the deeper mysteries of existence.

In essence, Tony's nomadic series serves as a testament to the enduring power of art to transcend cultural boundaries and connect us to the shared human experience. Through his evocative imagery and profound insights, he enjoins us to embark on a journey of exploration and discovery, where the boundaries between art and life blur, and the spirit of the Badjao people lives on in all its beauty and complexity.

In Tony's artistic repertoire, his portrayal of cats emerges as a captivating exploration of form, color, and symbolism. Through his geometric abstraction techniques, Tony transforms these familiar feline figures into dynamic compositions that go beyond traditional representations.

At the heart of Tony's fascination with cats lies a deep appreciation for their inherent grace, agility, and enigmatic presence. Through his geometric abstraction, he distills the essence of these creatures into their fundamental shapes and patterns and captures their essence with precision and elegance.

Each stroke of Tony's brush reveals the intricate geometry of the cat's form, from the graceful arc of its back to the sinuous curves of its tail, even re- positioning it in the front. For the non-artist, it is difficult to find the representations of the anatomy. One has to have a background in analytical cubism.

Through a careful interplay of lines and angles, he creates a sense of movement and vitality and imbues his feline subjects with a sense of life and energy that eclipses the static nature of the canvas.

Moreover, Tony's portrayal of cats serves as a metaphor for the human experience and calls viewers to contemplate themes of independence, curiosity, and the duality of nature. Through his abstract interpretations, he explores the complex interplay between order and chaos, structure and spontaneity and beckons us to reflect on our own relationships with the world around us.

In essence, Tony's cats represent a harmonious fusion of artistry and imagination, a testament to his skill as both a painter and a storyteller. Through his evocative imagery and meticulous attention to detail, he allows us to enter into a world where the boundaries between reality and abstraction blur, and the beauty of the natural world is revealed in all its intricate complexity.

This journey is mirrored in the works of other Cebuano artists, each contributing a unique facet to the tapestry of Cebuano modernism. Sio Montera, for instance, allows 'form' to emerge from the process itself, asking viewers to develop their perceptions and aesthetic feelings. His approach contrasts with Tony's detailed depiction of the Badjao, where we clearly see his emphasis the spontaneity and emergent qualities of abstract art. Montera's technique can be seen as a modernist response to traditional forms, where the process is as significant as the outcome and highlights the fluidity and dynamism of Cebuano art.

On the other, Karl Roque's works always reflect his love and concern for the environment present another dimension. Roque's art is deeply rooted in the Cebuano landscape and captures the natural beauty and environmental issues of the region. His focus on environmental themes contrasts with Tony's cultural and historical focus, yet both artists reflect a deep connection to their Cebuano heritage through their chosen themes.

Meanwhile, Gil Maningo's caricature painting and photography revolve around his faith and the use of gold leaf as his primary medium. Maningo's use of gold leaf resonates with the spiritual and religious themes in Tony's work, such as the depiction of Sto. Niño and San Pedro Calungsod. However, Maningo's style is more reflective of personal faith and the ornate tradition of religious art and provides a contrasting yet complementary perspective on Cebuano spirituality.

Boy Kiamko has a different take on art. His interspersing technique, which crosses other borders and breaks the continuity of lines, embraces the possibility of hues overshadowing one another. This technique contrasts with Tony's structured geometric abstraction but shares a common thread of exploring form and color to convey deeper meanings. Kiamko's work highlights the experimental spirit within Cebuano modernism, pushing boundaries and challenging conventional artistic norms.

Lastly, Jose Mari Picornell does not paint anything new. His subjects must be old for him to capture them before they vanish or are replaced with modern structures. Picornell's dedication to preserving the old contrasts with Tony's modernist approach but underscores a common Cebuano desire to connect with and preserve their shared cultural heritage.

Tony's work is part of a broader Cebuano modernist movement that includes notable names like Javy Villacin, Jojo Sagayno, Reynan Dingal, Alyssa Selanova, Khriss Bajade, Gerald Pongase, Joseph Ong, Pierre Famador II, Anthony Fermin, Ritchie Quijano, Wenceslao Cuevas, and the late Vidal, Jr. "Ondo" Alcoseba, Tony's brother. Each of these artists, through their exploration of abstract and modernist styles, adds a unique voice to the collective Cebuano narrative that enriches the cultural landscape with their individual perspectives and innovations.

The essence of Cebuano modernism in art lies in its unique synthesis of traditional influences and modernist experimentation. Artists like Tony Alcoseba, Sio Montera, Karl Roque, Gil Maningo, Boy Kiamko, Jose Mari Picornell and countless other Cebuano artists, each contribute to this narrative through their distinct approaches. Tony's exploration of the Badjao culture, combined with his geometric abstraction, exemplifies a blend of historical and modernist perspectives. Montera's process-focused abstraction, Roque's environmental themes, Maningo's religious iconography, Kiamko's experimental techniques, and Picornell's preservation of the old all highlight different facets of the development of the Cebuano art scene.

Together, these artists create a rich, multifaceted portrayal of Cebuano art, where tradition meets innovation, and personal narratives intersect with collective heritage. This convergence of diverse styles and themes underlines what makes Cebuano modernism uniquely dynamic, reflective of a culture that is both deeply rooted in its history and continuously evolving in response to contemporary influences. In Tony's works, we see the culmination of these influences. Tony's art embodies the spirit of Cebuano modernism in a way that is both deeply personal and universally resonant.

This solidifies his place and stature as an artistic game-changer as a uniquely Cebuano artist .

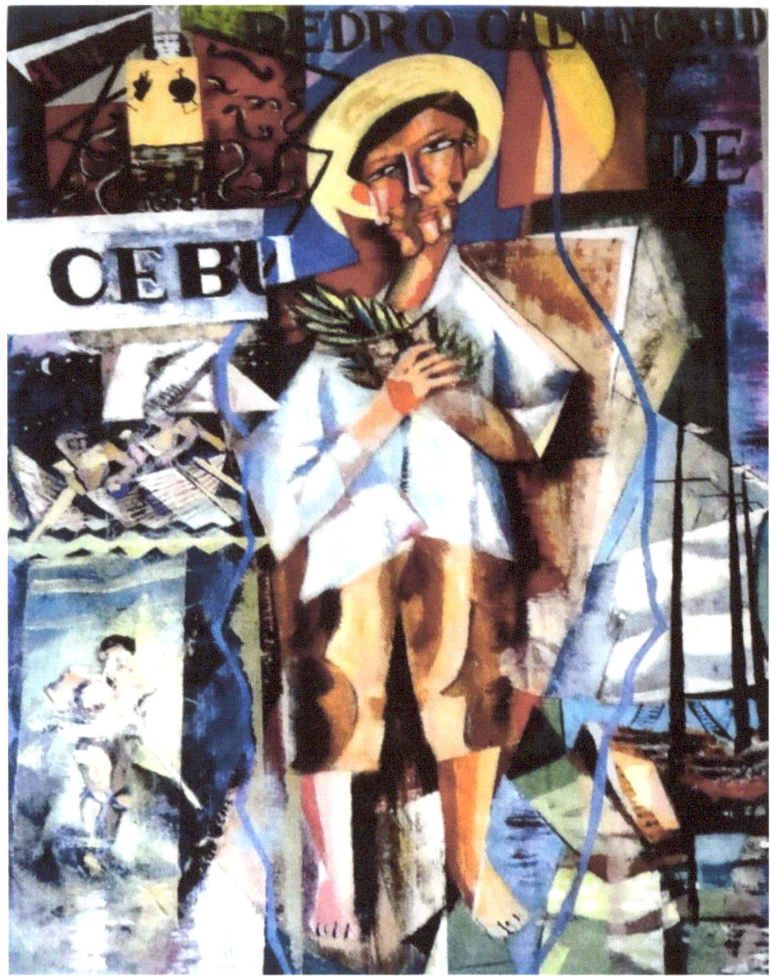

San Pedro Calungsod, 2012, 12 x 18 in, acrylic on canvas, digital print.

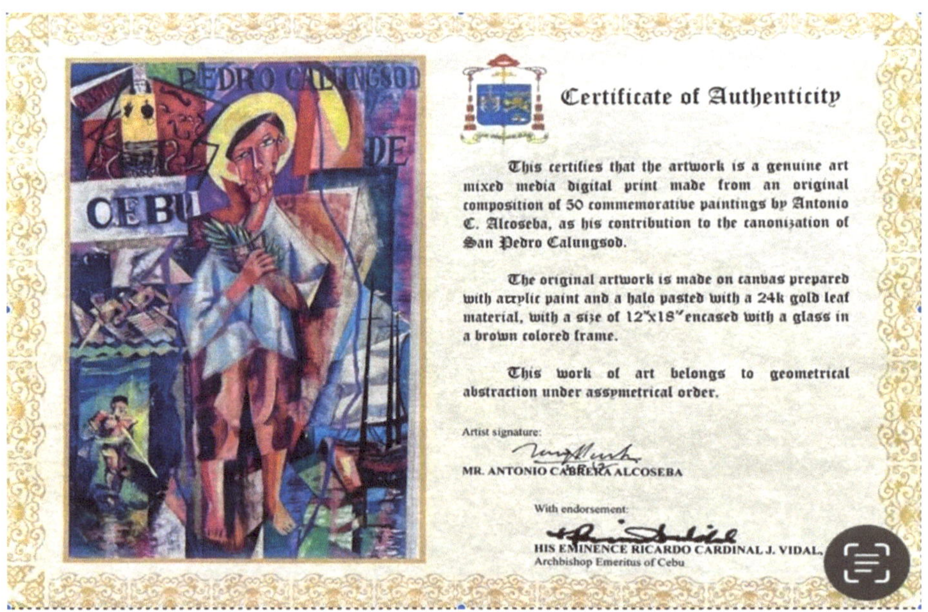

Certificate of Authenticity, Ricardo Cardinal Vidal's signature.

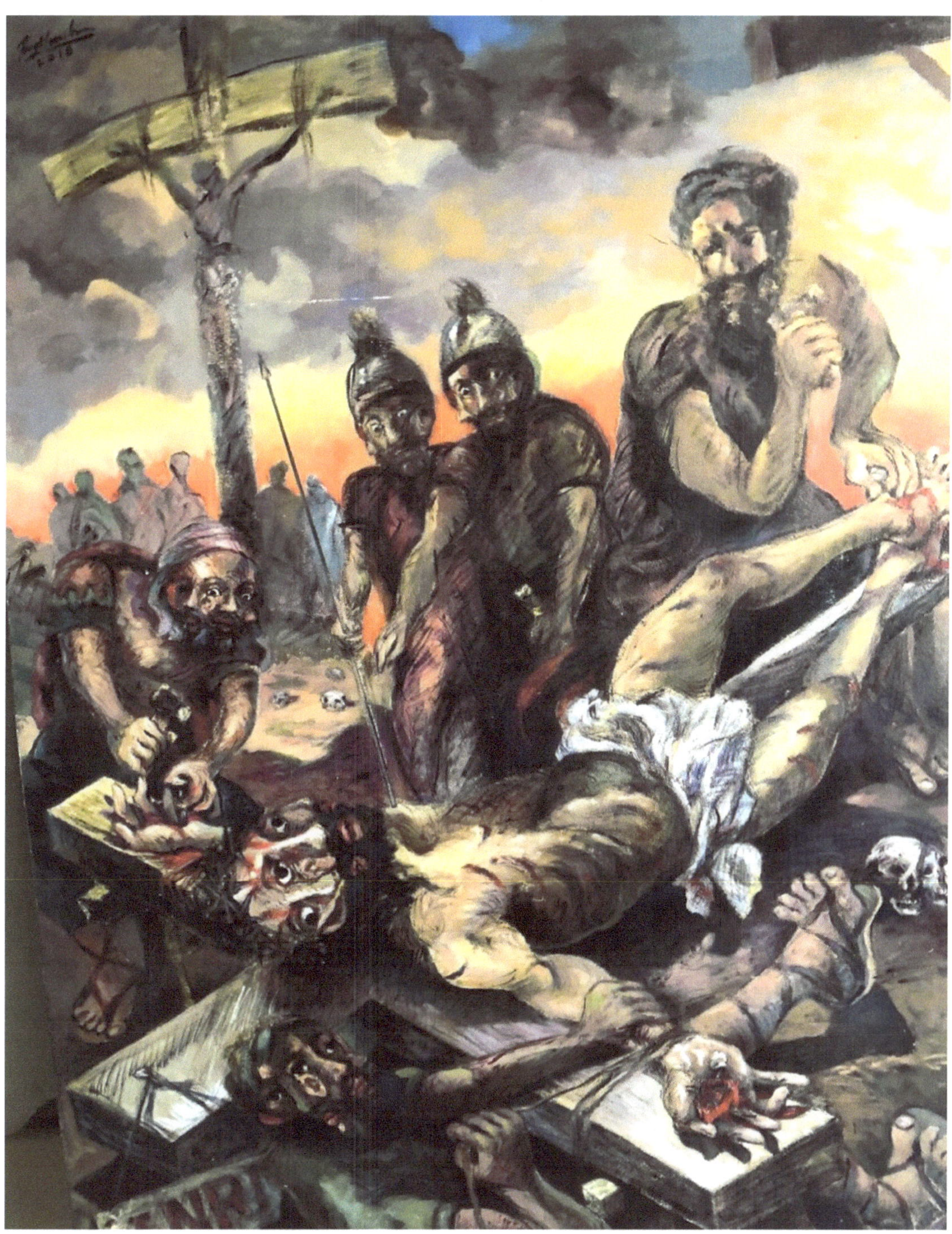

Cruxificion 2018, 4 x 4 ft, acrylic on canvas.

ACKNOWLEDGMENT

I would like to begin by expressing my gratitude to the artist Tony Alcoseba for sharing his artwork with me and allowing me to see things that are not typically visible. I am appreciative of the numerous informal interviews, some of which took place during unconventional times, and for providing me with access to pictures and artworks to which I would not have otherwise had access.

I would also like to extend my thanks to his sons, particularly Vanni and Dionnel, for their patience and assistance in collating, organizing, and providing photos and information on the dates, and dimensions of the paintings. Not all collectors could be listed individually, but their support and assistance are deeply appreciated.

Additionally, I am grateful for their efforts in obtaining permission from private collectors. Without their help, compiling such a vast collection of paintings into a book would have been considerably more challenging.

Lastly, I wish to express my appreciation to all collectors of Tony Alcoseba's paintings and patrons for granting permission to include their artwork in this book including whose names may have not been mentioned here.

BIBLIOGRAPHY

Artsper. "Tony Alcoseba." Accessed May 13, 2023. https://www.artsper.com/au/contemporary/philippines/97974-tony-alcoseba.

Chavez, R., and X. Yrastorza. *ALCOSEBA: Crossroads*. Cebu, Philippines: Qube Gallery, 2015.

Cramer, C., and K. Grant. "Georges Braque and Pablo Picasso: Two Cubist Musicians." Smarthistory. Accessed May 13, 2023. https://smarthistory.org/georges-braque-pablo-picasso-two-cubist-musicians.

Compendium of Essays from the Exhibition "Ginto": 50 Years of the Arts Association of the Philippines. Tall Galleries, Metropolitan Museum of Manila, November 10, 1998–January 24, 1999.

Düchting, Hajo. *Pablo Picasso*. Munich: Prestel Verlag, 2008.

Frascina, Francis, and T. Grabs, et al. *Modernity and Modernism: French Painting in the Nineteenth Century (Modern Art Practices and Debates)*. New Haven, CT: Yale University Press, 1993.

Greenberg, Clement. *Art and Culture: Critical Essays*. Boston: Beacon Press, 1989.

Jore, Jocelyn, ed. *Bantugang Sugbuanon: Arts and Artists of Cebu*. FSI Cultural Heritage Series, vol. 14, 2022.

Fernandez, Raymund. *Kamingaw: An Impressionist Portrait of the Bisaya Painter Martino A. Abellana*. Cebu City, Philippines: University of San Carlos Press, 2017.

Sadler, M. T. H., trans. *Concerning the Spiritual in Art* by Wassily Kandinsky. Garden City, NY: Dover Publications, 1977.

Stein, Gertrude. *Pablo Picasso*, 1874–1946. Mineola, NY: Dover Publications, 1984.

Palermo, Charles, et al. *Picasso and Braque: The Cubist Experiment, 1910–1912*. Fort Worth, TX: Kimbell Art Museum.

Pantaleon, C. E. "USJ-R Recognizes Families of Distinction." *The Philippine Star*, August 21, 2012. Accessed May 14, 2023. https://www.philstar.com/cebu-news/2012/08/21/840529/usjr-recognizes-families-distinction.

INDEX